Riding the Waves of Life

Riding the Waves of Life

Tom Eggum

LONGWOOD
COMMUNICATIONS

Published by:
Longwood Communications
397 Kingslake Drive
DeBary, FL 32713
904-774-1991

To order additional copies or to contact Tom Eggum to
speak to your group write:

Tom Eggum Communications
P.O. Box 5268
Glendale, AZ 85312
602-978-1719

Acknowledgments

I wish to thank some very special people who have made the writing and publishing of this book possible.

First of all, I'd like to thank **Doug Haugen,** who encouraged me to write this book and helped me get it off to a start. His friendship and encouragement mean so much to our ministry.

Also, I'd like to thank **Michelle Halonen,** my personal administrator, for her tireless work on this manuscript. Her commitment to our ministry is not only appreciated but vital to its life.

Also, **Kristi Howell,** for her insight and re-editing ability. We are grateful to her for her special part in this book.

Gary and Lios Hansen have been such a blessing

during the publishing process, and they share our desire to reach young people with the hope of Jesus Christ.

My Family is the most important part of my life. They make ministry so enjoyable by being so supportive and encouraging, even though I am away from home quite often. We make up for it during the times I am home by creating many family traditions. I love them so much.

Contents

Riding the Waves of Life

L ife is like the waves of the surf reaching the coastline. Sometimes they have a gentle, rolling action that is very soothing. Other times, a storm can churn the ocean's waters into dangerous, pounding waves, often bringing destruction to any person or thing in their path. Like the sometimes gentle, sometimes raging surge of the ocean's tides, life too has its ups and downs, its moments of triumphs and discouragement, and its times of joy and sadness.

This book is about facing life's difficulties and riding the rough seas of life, as well as enjoying the times of success and joy. You will identify with some of the stories told in the following pages; you will also find encouragement and hope. They are stories of people who have faced the storms of life and ridden out the waves. They not only survived but found strength and learned valuable lessons, inspiring them and others to live life to its fullest.

I have been close to death. I have also experienced the best life has to offer. I have met rich and poor in over fifty-five countries. I have seen the results of natural disasters and witnessed man's cruelty to man in politics and personal relationships. Yet, in spite of all that I have seen and experienced, I remain an optimist. I have found that there is good in most every situation. My life is filled with enthusiasm and hope. I enjoy life and I love to experience the best it has to offer. I love life! I am free!

However, my enthusiasm for life is not the result of position or possessions. My optimism is a result of my relationship with Jesus Christ. He is the Source that gives me strength in times of weakness, courage in times of discouragement, and hope in times of hopelessness. Without Jesus Christ, there is no story to be told.

Chapter One

FREEDOM

The world changed on November 22, 1963. When it was announced that President Kennedy had been assassinated, the world seemed to stand still—and then it changed, or at least it seemed to. I began to realize there are tragedies in life, and life is not always fair.

Leaders such as John and Bobby Kennedy and Dr. Martin Luther King, Jr. impacted the human rights movement and led many people in the United States to realize freedom. But there are still many in America and throughout the world who long for freedom. I found a greater appreciation for our freedom through my involvement with people who have none.

In 1988, I had been chosen to be one of the speakers for a national gathering of Christians at the

Washington Mall in our nation's capital. To my left was the Washington Monument, to my right the nation's Capitol. As I stood to speak in the shivering April rain, I turned toward the Lincoln Memorial and thought of all the historic speeches that had been made there. Many of those great speakers cried out for freedom from many forms of injustice.

One of those people was Dr. Martin Luther King, Jr., who in that same spot spoke to over a quarter of a million people who were struggling for civil rights.

"I have a dream," he said, "that one day my children will not be judged by the color of their skin but by the content of their character."

He concluded his speech by sharing his dream that one day "all of God's children would be able to say in the words of the old hymn, 'Free at last! Free at last! Thank God Almighty, I'm free at last!'"

All I could think was, *Who am I to be standing here?* Well, I'm not Martin Luther King, but I do share his dream. As insignificant as I felt, I put my face to the cold April rain and spoke to the people who were gathered there on behalf of those who could not speak for themselves.

Those who live under governments that do not allow them to protest their condition cry for freedom. Teenagers gripped by addiction, loneliness, and suicidal tendencies cry for freedom. Those who want to know whether their lives have purpose cry for freedom.

My personal search for freedom was a painful struggle. I grew up with a person I hated—myself. My outlook on life was very negative, and my life was a constant battle with depression and anger. Many times I did not believe life was worth living. I was convinced that I was of no value. In my anger, I lashed out at my parents, teachers, and anyone in authority. I poisoned those around me with my hatred; but my life was changed as I heard the voices of a group of college students who took an interest in me. They were rehearsing in my hometown of Thompson, Iowa, before they left on an east coast tour. Along with my friends, I attended their concert only to mock and curse them as they sang. In spite of my behavior, their message was not one of condemnation but of compassion—even for me.

Though I didn't trust them, their message was so positive that part of me wanted to know more. They took an interest in me and shared God's love with me. No matter what I said to them, they didn't give up on me; they helped me to realize that I wasn't a loser.

Through the people in this music group, I learned that I was valuable. I was someone special, not because of anything I had done but because I was loved by God. As a result of their faithfulness in reaching out to me, I have devoted my life to sharing the love of God with young people around the world. Because of my difficult youth, I can relate to the struggles teenagers must face, and I can encourage them as they find their place in this world.

In 1988, when I returned to my hometown to speak at an assembly on "positive image" at my old high school, the principal introduced me as "the person least likely to return and talk about anything positive!"

His introduction was a reminder of my negative attitude and the pain I had once caused other people. How gratifying it was to deliver a positive message where I had once brought such destruction.

I enjoy being able to motivate young people who feel like failures and to give them a message of encouragement and hope.

Since 1973, I have been involved in sharing a message of hope with the people of the former Soviet

Union. I have been deeply inspired by a number of people I met there, especially during the years of communism, when the people lacked even basic freedom.

Natasha was a young Russian whose life was an inspiration to me. As a young girl, she had been beaten, slapped by her teachers, and laughed at by her classmates for talking about Jesus. Her father had been arrested for sharing his faith in Christ. Natasha and her family endured all of this and more because they would not turn their backs on Jesus Christ, instead they proclaimed their faith in a country where it was not permitted.

Since the day I met her in a Moscow church, I have witnessed Natasha's deep, abiding faith. She was mature in faith beyond her thirteen years, and her struggle continued for many years. She told me of the persecution she and her father faced day after day.

As a young man, her father had studied Marxism at the University of Moscow, writing award-winning papers on the lives of Marx, the father of communism, and Lenin, the Soviet revolutionary leader When he read a propaganda magazine strongly criticizing Christians for their faith, he began to wonder whether they might have something worth believing in. His curiosity led him to study the life of Christ. This search led him to believe that Jesus was the Son of God, and he put his trust in Him.

From then on, his family was harassed for their faith in Jesus Christ. In spite of harassment from her classmates and her teachers, Natasha learned early to take a stand for her belief in God.

Natasha is one of the most positive people I've ever met. How can anyone who has gone through so much still express such joy in the Lord?

"When they beat me," she said, "I pray that they

will see the love of Jesus in me so they, too, can meet Him and have eternal life...All they have left to do now is take away my papa, but they'll never take away my faith in Jesus."

I kept in touch with Natasha and her father over the years and was greatly encouraged by their strong faith in spite of overwhelming persecution. They were actively engaged in helping other Christians who had suffered great loss. When I visited them in 1988, they told stories of how the police had continued to harass them. Their apartment was set on fire, rocks were thrown at Natasha's father, and the KGB accused Natasha of being a prostitute. Despite the hardship in their own lives, their great concern was for believers in prison who needed food, blankets, and warm coats. They were especially concerned for the Christians who had survived the nuclear reactor accident at Chernobyl. They referred to the survivors there as the "living dead," believing that thousands will die from radiation in the years to come. Natasha's father died just before the days of openness and greater religious freedom came to the Soviet Union. Shortly before the Communist government fell in August 1991, Natasha was able to immigrate to France, where she was finally free to enjoy freedom for the first time.

In 1961, a wall was built across the city of Berlin, Germany. The wall was built by the Communist East German government to keep its citizens from escaping to West Germany, where they could find freedom. Families were divided by this wall, never to see each other again. In the nearly thirty years that the Berlin Wall stood, dozens of people were killed by guards as they attempted to gain their freedom on the other side of the wall. In 1989, man's heartfelt desire for freedom did what bombs could not do—tore the wall down!

I revisited that wall in the fall of 1991 and stood in

the former "no-man's land," looking up at the Brandenburg Gate. I thanked God that freedom had finally ripped that terrible wall down, brick by brick.

I sympathize with those living under oppressive regimes, but I also grieve for people enslaved in other ways. Our *personal* freedom is not really dependent on the government or conditions under which we live but on our relationship to our Creator. Some of the truly free people I have met are living in Communist China, South Africa, and the former Soviet Union. Ironically, I have met some slaves living in the United States. You need to ask yourself, who or what is it that controls you? What is it that occupies your thoughts most of your waking hours? It is easy to be a slave to possessions, position, greed, selfishness, desires, or addictions. The Bible declares that unless we become slaves to Jesus Christ, we will never know true freedom. Natasha and her father truly found that freedom; so can you.

A man standing in front of a popular Moscow bookstore asked me, "Would you trade some of your clothes?" I have often been approached by young Russian people who want to practice English or trade things. I had nothing to trade, but we started to talk. His name was Igor, and he really became excited when he found out I was from Phoenix, Arizona. Igor was in the process of immigrating to the United States, and he hoped to live in Phoenix! Ever since he was in grade school, Igor had dreamed of one day living in a place where he can believe what he chooses and speak freely. There had been life-sized portraits of Lenin in his elementary school classrooms, and when he would express free ideas, his teachers would remind him how disappointed "father" Lenin would be.

Because Igor was very curious about God, he attended services in the Ukrainian Orthodox Church;

but when he asked his schoolteachers to help him believe in God, he was always criticized for his "foolishness."

While in college, he finally met someone who could help him. The more he questioned, the more his search for freedom and his dream of coming to a free society intensified. He is now living in the United States, and this is how he describes his new life: "I experience more freedom in one day than my friends (at home) dream of in a lifetime. Some days, I experience too much freedom...so I have to stay in my apartment!"

Igor now has freedom of expression as well as freedom of the heart. But his freedom started in his heart, and now his challenge is learning how to use that freedom.

In September 1988, I traveled with some friends—Mark, Bruce, Todd, and Scott—to China. We picked up our Christian literature from Asian Outreach Ministry in Hong Kong and safely entered China through customs in Shanghai, our contraband literature intact. While in Shanghai, we enjoyed an atmosphere of freedom as we passed out Christian literature unhindered, and we witnessed openly in parks. This was my sixth visit to China, and the liberty and newly found freedom I saw and experienced was exhilarating. A fifteen-year-old boy, who had just entrusted his life to Christ through a radio broadcast from Hong Kong, received a Bible from Scott.

A few days later we flew to Beijing, the capital of China. Beijing is the seat of the Communist government and has a reputation for being colder and stricter than the other cities. I warned my friends that we might not experience the freedom we had in Shanghai.

The rain drizzled down during our first night in

Beijing, but in spite of the weather, we went to Tiananmen Square. The few people there gladly took our Christian literature, and several chased us into a nearby subway station to get more. As we handed out booklets on the subway, the people were curious and excited to get the material, just as they had been in Shanghai.

Our hearts were light from the openness we sensed, and we laughed all the way to the hotel. We were delighted by the new liberties we were experiencing in a country once so closed to the Word of God.

The next night, everything changed. After a late dinner (Peking Duck—what else?) I returned to the hotel while my friends went back to Tiananmen Square to witness to more people.

This time, there was a different atmosphere. The people weren't as friendly as they had been the night before, and they appeared nervous. As Mark handed some Gospels to a few young people, a young man grabbed one and sped off on his bicycle. He returned with a number of uniformed police officers, who arrested Mark and Scott and shoved them into a police van. Although Todd and Bruce saw the commotion and the flashing lights of the van, they were unaware their friends had been arrested. However, soon they too were surrounded by policemen, arrested, and taken to the police station within the walls of the Forbidden City in Beijing.

My four friends were thoroughly questioned and forced to fill out forms admitting their guilt. Finally, they were escorted back to the hotel, forced to surrender their passports and remaining literature, and told to appear the next morning for their trial and sentencing.

The trial was swift, as most trials in China are. If

you are arrested, you are guilty. The four were ordered to pay a fine of two-hundred yuan and write a "new attitude paper" promising they would not commit a crime like this again. They were released and ordered not to interfere ever again with the beliefs of anyone within China.

That evening, I took a taxi to the other side of town where I could get rid of my literature before it was confiscated. I stood in the shadows of trees in a major park, praying that God would work through this situation. Because young people walked through this park as they left a local disco, all of my literature was distributed within a few minutes. Once again, God's Word had reached hungry people. Even the police chief and his officers had some of the literature.

In June 1989, when I heard the news of the massacre in Tiananmen Square, I couldn't hold back the tears. The students who had been demonstrating in the square were simply fighting for basic freedoms. They wanted to be able to express their religious and political beliefs; but instead, machine-gun fire silenced several thousand of them that terrible night. I remembered the students we had witnessed to during the previous year in that same square, and I was horrified as I watched the television reports of the massacre. The "People's Army" moved in with heavy artillery and piled bodies in the streets. Afterward, the government completely denied taking that action.

Just as the students in China were protesting in hopes of obtaining freedom, many are now searching for that freedom.

While on an outreach trip to the Soviet Union, my friends Dawn, Dave, Donna, and I met two people who were searching. One thought we were lying to him when we tried to share the freedom of God's love with him.

Serge was a young Russian student who earned a living by trading with foreigners on the streets of Moscow. When I gave him a book entitled *Evolution vs. Creation*, he looked at it and told me the story of Creation was a lie. I told Serge his professors were the ones who had lied to him, and that he was created by a loving God, who cared deeply for him and had a special purpose for his life.

The skeptic in him melted as he began to read the book and think about what I said to him. Like a flower opened to the rain, his heart was opened more and more as he asked questions about Jesus. When he brought home the Bible I had given him, his grandmother's eyes welled with tears. She was a life-long believer but had never owned a Bible.

Ludmilla was another young Russian who was longing for peace and freedom. We met her in a park in Leningrad, where I gave her a Russian gospel booklet titled *Satan or Jesus Christ*. As she began to read, she said that she had never heard of Jesus Christ. She told us how empty she and many of her friends were because of the hardships they faced. We knew she needed God's love in her life, so we began to explain who Jesus is and how He loves and cares for her. She seemed to grasp some of His compassion as I shared how He had changed my life.

When my wife, Diane, and I traveled to South Africa several years ago, we found the local people to be very outgoing, and we quickly made friends with some of them. However, we were bewildered by the restrictions of apartheid. Because of this unjust system, we could not eat with our new friends at a local restaurant, play on the same golf course, or even go to the beach with some of them because of the color of their skin. The white minority government would not allow me to say anything about the system, even while speaking in churches. I was angry and frustrated. We were not free to enjoy time with our friends, and I was not free to preach what God had laid on my heart.

When freedom comes to a nation that has been under an oppressive government, it is breathtaking. I was speaking at a youth leadership conference in Oradea, Romania, a few months after the fall of Nicolae Ceausescu, the feared Communist dictator. Doug Tegnor (a national youth leader) and I were staying in a small flat with a Romanian family. One day, Yuri, our host, was telling us about the day of Ceausescu's fall from power. He told of hearing the radio announcement that there was an emergency and everyone was ordered to stay in their homes. He listened to music being played over the radio for several hours. Then another announcement was given—Ceausescu had fled. Yuri said he needed to celebrate with others, so he took the tram to the center of the city. Already, seventy thousand people had gathered in front of the Communist headquarters. When the announcement was given over the loudspeakers that the dictator had been overthrown, there was incredible joy in that square. Yuri said it was the most joyful moment in his life. Everyone was hugging one another and crying tears of joy. "Then," Yuri said, "everyone dropped to their knees and began reciting the Lord's Prayer and saying 'Our God is great!' " Freedom had come to Romania. The people could openly discuss their God!

I had the privilege of being in Moscow a few days after the attempted coup and fall of communism in August 1991. From my hotel window, I could see the burned-out buses and barricades surrounding the Russian parliament building. My friend Misha was one of the thousands of Russians who had formed a human barrier around the parliament building to protect

President Yeltsin from the Soviet army tanks surrounding the building. Late one night, Yeltsin had received word that the KGB and the Soviet Army were going to attack the parliament building by crushing the people and blowing the bottom floors out of the building. The plan was to arrest Yeltsin. Misha had to make a decision when they were told of the possibility of attack that night. He decided to defend freedom, even if it meant dying. Several brave Russians did die that evening, but the soldiers who manned the tanks turned their guns away from the building and refused to fire on their own people. The coup failed, and the Soviet Union was dissolved a few days later. Freedom had finally come after over seventy years of communism!

In the following days, I was a speaker for the "Moscow Gospel Music Festival." Our team spoke and sang in the streets, parks, theaters, schools, and prisons of Moscow. Thousands of Russian people freely heard the good news of Jesus Christ. They were very open to hearing the message of freedom that Jesus Christ offers. The Russian people almost bombarded us to get the literature. As we stood in the square with the Bibles, we were able to give away over 150,000 New Testaments in just ten days.

The highlight of my life happened on September 5 during that trip to Moscow. I had the opportunity to join the Holy Smoke Band as they put on a concert at a Moscow public school. I asked the school principal what I would be allowed to share with the students. I'll never forget his response. He said, "Atheism has left our students bankrupt. Please tell them whatever you know about God." The band sang about Jesus Christ and how He helps us through life's problems, and I spoke openly about God and His love for the students. Their response was enthusiastic and eager. Every student and teacher received a New Testament. Their thirst for the Word could now be quenched legally, and they no longer feared the consequences of religion. I am still amazed at the great freedom and opportunity I had to share Christ openly in the schools throughout Russia. I only wish we had that same freedom in North America.

That evening, I spoke at the Children's Palace Theater. At the conclusion of the concert given by the Holy Smoke Band, Debbie Rieks (a former Miss America runner-up) and the band First Love, I gave a message about the hope we have in our relationship with Jesus Christ. When I asked for those who wanted to know Jesus and give their lives to Him to stand, I was amazed. Tears poured down my face as I watched most of the people rise to their feet. Within minutes, people were coming to me and telling me how they had just given their lives to Jesus. Among them was a Navy officer who said, "I just stood to give my life to Jesus, and I want to hug you." I'll never forget that hug.

In 1992, I was able to return to Russia five different times to preach and lead outreach teams. I never thought I would see the day when it was easier to speak about Jesus in Russia than in North America.

During the autumn of 1992, I was speaking with the outreach "Mission Volga." One night while speaking at an outdoor event in the city of Volgograd, I sensed God's presence in a very powerful way as I spoke about freedom. Several hundred people had gathered around the stage to listen, and they seemed to take in every word. My interpreter was deeply touched by God's presence and the openness of the people. She said to me, "I am so touched that I have tears in my throat." A young man who had been cursing us at the beginning prayed to receive Christ into his life.

Afterwards, people crowded around the stage to ask questions. One older man questioned whether God could forgive every wrong we had committed. He said, "I want to believe you, but it is so difficult after having been told for the past seventy years that there is no God."

Victoria, my Russian translator, said it well: "We now have high inflation, shortages of work and food, but we have freedom—freedom to say whatever we wish, and to believe in Jesus Christ openly. It is worth the suffering to have freedom."

Freedom so often has a price. It is a very precious treasure, which I hold as one of the greatest gifts from God. The Bible promises us true freedom through our relationship with Jesus Christ. He frees us from the guilt of failure and sin, and promises to love us through our most difficult times. In Galatians 5, verses 1 and 13, Paul tells us, "It is for freedom that Christ has set us free. Stand firm, then, and do not let yourselves be burdened again by a yoke of slavery...You, my brothers, were called to be free. But do not use your freedom to indulge the sinful nature; rather, serve one another in love."

Chapter Two

WHY?

If tragedy forces us to ask one question, it is *Why?* Why do thirty-eight thousand people have to die each day from starvation and malnutrition? Why do parents have to get divorced? Why do we all have struggles? Why is there so much suffering in the world? Why do people have to die?

I remember the feeling of shock and devastation when my thirteen-year-old nephew, Gary, was murdered by a fifteen-year-old friend. This friend, under the influence of drugs, took a loaded 38-caliber pistol, put it to Gary's head, and pulled the trigger. No one struggles with the unfairness of this more than my sister Judy (Gary's mother). There is no loss greater than the loss of your own child. When young people die, so do hopes for the future. A child dying before a parent is just not natural to us, and we are never prepared for it.

Dave Kamrath lost his father when he was in junior high. Dave has been my friend since high school, and now he is an associate of mine who speaks to students all over the world. I asked him to write in his own words about the pain he has faced in his life:

> I grew up on a farm in Wisconsin. My family life meant everything to me. My dad and my brother, Dan, were my closest friends. We worked, hunted, fished, talked, and played together.
>
> I could tell my dad anything and everything. My goal in life was to be like my dad and please him. If I thought something was important to him, or if he asked me to do something, I would do it with all my energy. There was no doubt that he loved me.
>
> I was called into the principal's office on the first day of school when I was thirteen. My two sisters and Mom were there crying, and our pastor was there too.
>
> Mom had difficulty blurting out that my dad had died. He had been working on his ultralight plane, and as he drove it down the runway to put it away, a cable snapped, causing it to take off. Another cable broke and the plane crashed. My insides convulsed as I tried to absorb the horror.
>
> "Where is he?" I demanded. "Let's go see him! I've got to go see my dad! I want to be there!"
>
> I did not want to believe what I was

hearing.

"We can't see him," my mom said again, "He died."

I became rigid. I couldn't believe it. It wasn't true. I looked at my pastor. I looked at the principal. I looked at my mom.

"No!" I shouted as I fled to my locker and sat, stupefied. *This can't be happening,* I thought. *It's a cruel lie!*

My best friend approached me and asked what was wrong. I clenched my fist. I wanted to grab him by the throat and scream, "Keep out of this! Shut your mouth!"

I struggled through that year, always missing my dad, always asking why. Then, my brother went to Japan to go to college. My mom, my sisters, and I moved to Phoenix. I was so alone, in a strange place. I had no friends, and I hung around with kids who drank, so I started getting drunk. I was so angry, and I often looked for fights.

Someone would ask, "Dave, why did you move here?"

Sometimes I would punch them. Inside I was the one who was crying. "It's none of your business!" I would always answer.

It's none of your business why I hurt. It's none of your business why I spend nights sobbing into my pillow.

I wanted help but didn't know how to get it. I wanted the love I had lost when my dad died, but I couldn't find it. The more I craved it, the angrier I got.

I lay awake nights wondering, *Why am I here? I used to live for my dad, but he's not here. My brother is in Japan. I have no reason to live.*

Mom would haul me to church. That's where I met Tom Eggum. Tom had a joy and love about him that I didn't understand. He, too, had experienced hatred and bitterness, and a feeling the world was against him, yet he had a love in his eyes that I couldn't turn away from.

After months of crying, questioning, and feeling angry, I finally understood. Tom had overcome pain and bitterness with the help of Jesus Christ. He told me that I could have that same help. It was a free gift from God.

"No way!" I protested. "God could never accept me after what I've done...the thoughts I've had...the people I've messed up. He could never accept me!"

Tom replied, "Dave, He can."

One night I was lying in bed crying—again. I'd gotten drunk, again, and gotten into a fight, again. I beat up a guy and left him in the gutter.

"God, if you're there," I pleaded, "help me. I want what Tom has. Lord, please change my life."

My life did not change dramatically.

Why?

> I didn't feel any different. I still
> struggled, and I still missed my dad,
> but slowly God showed me His love
> and acceptance. Now the love I had
> for my dad, I have for Jesus.

It would be unfair to say that when someone we love dies, the void left by that special person in our lives will be filled by another. That space will always be there. The loss of a family member or friend changes our lives forever.

God promises us that He will walk through the valley of the shadow of death with us. We walk through all the stages of grief, including denial and anger. When we come out on the other side, the void is not filled, but the pain is bearable.

My friend Doug also experienced the death of a young person very close to him. When he was sixteen years old, his best friend, J.R., died. He remembers how this affected J.R.'s parents. I asked Doug to write these next paragraphs in his own words.

> I hurt, but I don't think anyone could
> hurt as much as J.R.'s parents did.
>
> Most of us think we're going to live
> forever when we are young, or at least
> another sixty years. We assume our
> friends are going to live with us. The
> death of a friend brings us face to face
> with our own mortality.
>
> I remember hiding my face, hoping
> they would say they were just kidding.
> I thought, *What a cruel joke!* but it
> wasn't a joke at all. It was like
> someone hit me; I was in a daze. I
> didn't really cry (at first).

For the next year, I just didn't want to believe it. I'd never hurt like that before...I'd never hurt so much inside—I'd never cried so much in my entire life. I knew that J.R. was in heaven, but it still didn't make my pain go away. I don't think I could have made it without my friends. The first month was the hardest—it's easier now. I can talk about him and not cry. When someone you care about dies, you change, you feel an emptiness inside you; it's like someone has cut something off from you and you'll never get it back.

Jackie was an attractive sixteen-year-old girl who was very outgoing. She attended a local Christian school and was a regular member of our youth group. One night, the car in which Jackie was riding pulled into the path of another car. They were hit head-on, and her life ended. Some of us had seen her just hours before, full of the life that was now snuffed out. Her death had a great impact on many of the young people in our youth ministry. Each of us was faced with the stark reality that there is no guarantee we will live a long life.

A few short weeks later, another member of our youth group was killed in an accident involving a drunk driver. Once again, we were faced with the question of why.

I have faced the deaths of family members and young people around me. Many of my friends have also lost loved ones. These experiences are devastating, but though it seems your life can't go on, it does; and Jesus is always there to get you through such times.

My sister loved Bob, and he loved her. Marriage was in their future. Bob had fought many battles in his life, including alcoholism. With the help of Alcoholics Anonymous, he had been sober for five years. When he began to experience memory lapses, Bob underwent tests to determine the cause. A brain tumor was discovered.

After much prayer, he made the difficult decision to have the tumor surgically removed. He told my sister many times that he had confidence that his life was in Jesus' hands. No matter what happened, he believed God was in control. Bob called my sister from his Los Angeles hospital bed before surgery to tell her he loved her and said, "Remember, Honey, no matter which way it goes, I'll be okay."

The next phone call my sister received was from the doctor. A blood vessel had burst during the surgery. The trip from our home in Phoenix to Los Angeles was never longer. When we arrived at the hospital, we were told that Bob probably would not live. If he did, he would need total care the rest of his life. We prayed and hoped for a miracle. Six days later we said good-bye, and Bob went to be with Jesus.

Anger is a part of grief. My sister was angry and bitter toward God. She had approached God in every way she knew and thought He had let her down; but I watched as she moved toward healing, and the trust she has for God is now deeper than ever. She has a ministry with a special sensitivity for others who are grieving.

There is no easy answer to why tragedies happen. You and I know people who deal every day with a life-threatening illness, unfair treatment at home, or untimely death, and we continue to ask why.

Almost daily, I am asked these types of questions

by family members, friends, and people I meet around the world. I do not have the answers to their specific questions, but I do know that Jesus Christ can truly heal our wounds and give us the strength and courage to go on. Through His love, I was able to overcome anger and hatred, my sister was able to accept Bob's death, and Dave was able to once again experience the love he had felt from his father.

God promises to be with us in those darkest hours. I recently saw a statement that I have found to be so true: "The Bible—it won't stop life's waves from crashing down on you, but it does teach you how to ride them."

Chapter Three

ANSWERING THE CRY
OF THE HURTING

Tim was no wimp. He was built like a professional wrestler. The first time I met Tim, he was in tears.

"My dad is an alcoholic, and he hits me a lot. Would you give me a hug? *I just want a hug,*" he said. As he wrapped his arms around me, I was struck with how simple it is to show someone we care. Tim was strong; he nearly broke my ribs! It wasn't the first hug I had given that spoke louder than words.

The most memorable hug I've ever given happened when I spoke at a series of meetings held in a tent in the city of Port Elizabeth, South Africa. Each night, many people came to see what was going on in the tent. One night as I began to preach, a little nine-year-old boy walked in. He was ragged and dirty. I immediately felt a deep love and compassion for him. I wanted to reach into the second row where he sat and hug him, even though he nodded off and slept through my entire sermon.

As I was greeting people at the back tent flap after the service, I saw him approaching. When I reached out to him, he ran, as if for his life.

I was later told that he was one of the hundreds of beggar children in this particular village. Their families are unable to feed them; they live on the streets and in the garbage.

Sleep came with difficulty that night. I kept seeing his face and praying for God to bring him back. The next night was a repeat of the first. He came, he sat, he fell asleep. I waited for him at the back of the tent, and even blocked the opening. When he came to the back, I grabbed him and started to hug him. I felt his little arms go around my back. He must have locked his hands together to get such a tight grip on me. His trembling soon stopped. No longer afraid, he hung on. Maybe it was his first hug.

I now had his trust, and I told him he could sleep in the tent where he would be safe. On the fourth night, he was wide awake to hear the message. When I invited people to come to the front and ask Jesus to come into their lives, he slipped from his seat and joined others at the front. He wanted to know Jesus, and he and I wept and hugged at the altar as we talked about Jesus Christ. I still have a picture of this little boy who is now a believer, and his eyes sparkle with joy. I believe a hug brought that little guy into the kingdom.

All across the world, but especially in North America, I am invited to speak in public schools on the topics of "Life with Value" and "Saying No to Drugs."

One school assembly had gotten off to a rough

start for me; a number of students were trying to disrupt me when I started to speak. The principal had warned me that, because of violence, this was the first assembly they had tried in two years. Once I identified the leaders and began to joke with them, it seemed that things went pretty well. As I continued to communicate to the nine hundred students about how special they were, telling them why and how to say no to drugs, their defenses came down and a strange wall of silence surrounded us. We all had a sense that something was going to happen, but we didn't know what. I told them that because we are each special people, we should look for ways to build one another up rather than put one another down.

The principal came to the podium to dismiss the students at the conclusion of my talk. He turned to me and asked, "Now what do we do?"

I responded, "Hug each other."

"Well, I might as well get it started!" he said.

With that, he gave the vice principal a hug! The students cheered!

Those young people were crying out to hear that they were valued. Many were in tears and lingered after the assembly, wanting to know how to deal with drug habits and thoughts of suicide.

When I returned a year later, one student told me that because of the assembly the year before, she had decided not to commit suicide.

While speaking at another high school assembly in Wisconsin, I invited students who were interested in hearing more to come to a church where I would be speaking that evening. Many students carpooled from nearby towns to hear more of what I had to say about the value of life. That evening I told them that in the schools, I had not been able to talk about Jesus Christ, the real Source of life. They listened closely as I shared the gospel, and at the conclusion of the evening meeting, I invited students to entrust their lives to the person of Jesus Christ. One student who asked Jesus to come into her life said her parents were surprised when she told them she was going to church that night, since she had never been to church before. When I asked whether I should write them a note to prove she was really in church, she responded that it wouldn't matter to them because when she left home that evening, they were smoking marijuana with her brother!

She was an example of many young people who have very little support from their parents. Though I was limited as to what I could say about God in the schools, somehow this young woman heard enough to know that she wanted to hear more. She knew that she was looking for meaning in her life. Now she had met the Author of life, Jesus Christ, and was beginning a new life of purpose. I met the girl about a year later, and she not only had lived a much fuller life but had shared her newfound purpose and joy for life with her family.

I was overwhelmed by the students' needs on those two campuses and by how open they were to talking about them. I hear the same cry for help on campuses everywhere I go, just different voices. I have a deep concern and love for the youth of today, and I am committed to being a positive influence in their lives. I wish I could paint a rosy, positive, enthusiastic "everything's going great, rah rah" picture of today's youth culture; but the truth is, many of our young people are hurting deeply. I don't believe there has ever been a generation of young people facing more pressure than today's youth. They are bombarded with negative messages on every side through music, television, movies, peers, and for many, their families.

According to one recent survey, the average high

school student hears sixteen negative comments about themselves before they hear one positive. It's not surprising that many young people feel bad about who they are!

With the breakdown of the family, young people are pressured to grow up fast. They are looking for secure, loving relationships—many times in the wrong places. Feelings of insecurity are fostered as the security of the home is threatened.

One student, commenting on his drug abuse, said, "If I can't feel significant, I want to at least feel good." With abuse and neglect on the rise, many students like this young man are turning to drugs, running away, or attempting suicide to escape their pain.

Renee, a thirteen-year-old, told me about drinking daily to deaden the pain of not being cared for by a workaholic father.

Kevin, a seventeen-year-old student, was following in his deceased mother's steps, practicing witchcraft. No one had ever told him that he was loved. I had the opportunity to share God's love with him. The pain came out in sobs too deep for words. Jesus knows the prayers in those sobs. The Bible tells us that Jesus himself "offered up prayers and petitions with loud cries and tears" (Heb. 5:7).

Julie had attempted suicide three times. She was twelve years old. Sometimes when she heard her parents fighting, she would just curl up in a ball and cry. She blamed herself for their problems and wondered if anyone really cared for her. She wondered why she should go on living.

As she and her mother were leaving my office, I asked if I could hug her. Her mother said that would be fine; her father refused to show any affection toward her.

Ann was crying for help when she came to my

office. She was the perfect example of a happy, healthy, middle-class teenager, but her new stepfather would not accept her. He finally made her live in the garage, leaving her food on the doorstep. After several days of being treated like a dog, she ran away and came to our local youth ministry. I was unsuccessful in trying to reconcile Ann with her family, and a number of weeks later she moved in with several young men. My heart ached because I had seen such tremendous potential in her which her parents had failed to notice. Ann's situation is more common than we would want to believe. As a youth minister in a suburban church, I once needed to find homes for five young people like Ann in a single week.

I have seen the fear and emptiness in the eyes of many American young people. I have seen it in rural areas as well as in major cities. I've seen the same look in the eyes of young people from the streets of Moscow and Leningrad to Shanghai and Beijing, to Cape Town and Tokyo. But never had I witnessed such fear and emptiness as I saw in a Cambodian refugee camp in Thailand.

I was on a special assignment, videotaping the work of a major worldwide relief organization. Thousands of people had flooded into this camp after the Vietnamese invasion of Cambodia. Seventeen thousand people were crammed into a four-block area. Many were children who had seen the rape and murder of family members as they fled their native country. They had already seen a lifetime of horror.

Early one morning as I stood in the makeshift bamboo food distribution center, I noticed the eyes of the children. Their hollow looks told of their desperate fear. They were hesitant to receive rice from the other workers and me. The last strange adults they had seen caused them to run for their very lives. Those strangers had raped their sisters and killed their parents. Why should they trust us? How long would it take for them, if they ever could, to trust someone who was genuinely concerned for them? It was beautiful to see caring, Christian young people showing the love of Jesus by distributing food, clothing, and blankets to these people. I witnessed the dispelling of fear through God's love.

The child that has had the greatest effect on my life is one whose eyes did not know fear; his mother's did. When I entered the mountain village of La Palma, El Salvador, a woman with a baby in her arms ran toward my interpreter and me. She held her baby out to me, and I innocently reached out to receive the baby. I assumed she wanted me to hold it or even pray for the child, but she was *giving* her child to me.

"Stop!" my friend shouted. He informed me that she wanted me to *keep* her baby and take the child to America. I had to turn my back. Walking away was one of the most difficult things I have ever done, but it would have been impossible for me to take the child. The cry of that desperate mother with her child still haunts me and is a constant reminder to me of the great need to be involved in the lives of people who are less fortunate. However, I've also discovered that people who seem to have it all, also have the same needs as everyone else.

Jeremiah 9:23–24 tells us, "Let not the wise man boast of his wisdom . . . or the rich man boast of his riches, but let him who boasts boast about this: that he understands and knows me, that I am the Lord."

You may have adopted your own philosophy about life. You may have said in your heart, *I have it together! I'm doing okay! I'm educated, I'm strong, I'm popular—I don't need God!*

If your trust is in your beauty, strength, or abilities,

be warned! Each of these things could be taken away from you in a moment.

There are many people in need of encouragement and attention. Not all of them are in third-world countries. Not all of them face firing squads because of their faith. Not all of them are young people with difficult family situations. Often, those who *seem* to have everything a person could want still struggle to fill an emptiness inside. These people may have a healthy family life, nice clothes, cars, and popularity, but there is still something missing.

There was a man who lived long ago who was a real "party animal." He was born in a royal palace and was supercharged with talent. He wrote over a thousand songs, was handsome, and was admired by women. He became a king, surrounded with luxuries, and had seven hundred wives. He also had three hundred girlfriends, four thousand vehicles, twelve thousand horses, tons of gold and silver, and he had fame. Kings and queens traveled hundreds of miles just to see him. He really knew how to have a good time.

He built an incredible temple and royal palace, and threw a party to celebrate it. He invited people from all over the world. They slaughtered twenty-two thousand cattle and fourteen thousand goats, and partied fourteen days straight. He would have been on "Lifestyles of the Rich and Famous" five times!!! But all of it left him empty.

This king of kings I've described was Solomon. He lived over 2,500 years ago. Solomon's emptiness came because he was looking for fulfillment in earthly pleasures rather than in the Lord's love for him. We are often tempted to believe that if we just had "a little more," we would be happy. The problem is that we follow our own sensual desires. Solomon lived for worldly pleasures and possessions rather than God's love and forgiveness and the knowledge that we have been created for a purpose.

Often, our pursuit of happiness and power leaves us empty and alone. An example of a lonely man who had it all was Howard Hughes. At the age of forty-five, Hughes was one of the wealthiest and most famous men in America. He dated actresses and many other famous women. He was a pilot and owned an airline and a string of hotels around the world. He was envied by people; he seemed to lack nothing.

Twenty years later, at sixty-five, he still had plenty of money—$2.3 *billion*! But the world's richest man had become one of the most pathetic. He lived in small dark rooms atop his luxury hotel. He was unkempt, with a waist-length beard and shoulder-length hair, and he weighed under one hundred pounds. He lay naked in bed, deathly afraid of germs. Life had no meaning. Emaciated and hooked on drugs, he died at the age of sixty-seven—alone.

Our society places high value on sensual pleasures, appearance, wealth, and the need to excel. Many young people feel it is necessary to pursue these things.

Dawn, a high-school student, got caught in this trap. She was attractive and popular, and was voted homecoming queen. One of her greatest attributes was her deep faith in Jesus Christ. She was not ashamed of it or afraid to share her faith with others. Gradually, however, she got caught up in her popularity and felt it necessary to be at the "right parties," and she started dating a young man who wanted nothing to do with God.

Dawn's young man soon became more important to her than her relationship with God, and she began to sense an emptiness in her life. When he broke up with her, it seemed to her that her life was shattered. She had given him everything, and she realized she meant nothing to him.

I was able to tell her that she still meant everything to God. God had not moved. God was waiting with open arms for her to come back into a relationship with Him. Like Solomon, Dawn "did not follow the Lord completely" (1 Kings 11:6).

When God created us, He did not intend for us to live on our own, separated from His love. He wants to be our best friend, our source of joy, and our reason to celebrate life.

According to Rabbi Harold Kushner in *When All You've Ever Wanted Isn't Enough*, "Our souls are not hungry for fame, comfort, wealth, or power. Our souls are hungry for meaning, for the sense that we have figured out how to live so that our lives matter, so that the world will be at least a little bit different for our having passed through it."

Psychologist Carl Jung, in *Modern Man in Search of a Soul*, once said, "About a third of my cases are suffering from no clinically defined neurosis, but from the senselessness and emptiness of their lives."

The prophet Jeremiah tells us that if we seek life in the world, it will leave us empty. "They have forsaken me, the spring of living water, and have dug their own cisterns, broken cisterns that cannot hold water" (Jer. 2:13). That is exactly what happens when we seek a life patterned after anything other than God's plan.

I remember hearing a story that paints a picture for us of how much Jesus identifies with us. It is a parable about the final day of judgment. A large mass of people stood on a great plain before God's judgment seat. The crowd was very angry with God.

A group of Jews who had suffered immense persecution, especially during World War II, stood.

"What can God know about our sufferings?" they cried. "We've been beaten and tortured to death."

Some African Americans in the crowd questioned God's right to judge them, considering the indignities of slavery and the second-class citizenship they had endured.

There were children born out of wedlock, children who did not know their ancestry, who also protested God's right to judge. The hungry, the homeless, the emotionally hurting, and the physically challenged also complained.

Each group decided to choose a leader. After the leaders met, they presented their case to God. They told God that before He could be qualified to be their judge, He must first endure the tests and trials they had endured. So this was their sentence: God must live on earth as a man with no special divine powers to cushion the hurts of life. He must be born a Jew and illegitimate, with His birth in question so that He can inherit nothing. He must be given a task so difficult that even His family will think Him mad. He must describe what is impossible to describe. He must describe God to humanity. He must be rejected and betrayed by His family and friends, indicted on false charges, and wrongly convicted. He must also be tortured and put to death in a horrible fashion.

Suddenly there was silence. No one spoke a word.

Each person realized that God had already served His sentence.

What is God like? Look at Jesus. He wants to answer that cry from our hearts. He is the God who has been where we are and experienced our hurts and sorrows. He is the God who loved us enough to suffer and die for us, so that we might have life through His incredible love.

Riding the Waves of Life

Chapter Four

MORE THAN A BATTLE

I have been arrested twice in my life. The first time was before I had a relationship with Jesus Christ. The charge was assault with a deadly weapon. The last time was for bringing Bibles and Christian literature into the Soviet Union.

The first time, I was the one full of hatred. While in a drunken rage, I began to argue with a friend and tried to kill him. I had done everything within my power to make life a living hell for those who cared the most for me. But my parents and the members of that music team had nothing but God's unconditional love for me.

The police officer who arrested me showed me a great amount of mercy. A few days after my arrest he said: "Tom, we have witnesses and your illegal gun.

There are a lot of people in this town that would like to see you spend time in jail. We have decided to put you on probation for two weeks. If you can behave yourself, we'll consider dropping the charges against you. We are turning your gun over to the state of Iowa as a confiscated illegal weapon, but your name will not be connected to it. If you prove trustworthy, you will have a clean police record."

Two weeks later, I watched Charlie tear up the charges and records that had been filed against me. The slate was clean. I had a new beginning with Christ and the law.

The last time I was arrested, I experienced the battle from the other side. My heart was full of love, and I had a great concern for those living under Soviet oppression; but I was arrested for attempting to bring Bibles into the Soviet Union. This time, it was I who faced an intense wall of hatred.

I waited in the cold, bare room to see what my destiny would be. To say I was afraid would be an understatement! I had brought Bibles and other Christian literature into the Soviet Union on a number of previous trips. I had made it safely before. Why was I subjected to this now? The first time I crossed the border in 1973, my van was left in a shambles by the guards when they searched it. They even ripped out the ceiling lining, yet failed to find the Bibles I had hidden in my clothing.

On another mission, I had flown to the Soviet Union with a tour group. As we boarded the Russian airliner in Amsterdam, the hand of the guard who frisked me hit a Bible. Instinctively I twisted just as his hand returned to the same place...to find my wallet. The two women before me were asked if they had any books or magazines. When I got to the customs desk in Leningrad, I was asked if I had any fruits or vegetables! I could honestly say no!

I had witnessed many miraculous border crossings. Why was I being arrested this time? Had I become overconfident in my own abilities? Had I done something that was not pleasing to God? Would I have been safe if I had more faith? Would I ever see my family again, or for that matter, my companion who had been taken to another room? What was going to happen to me? What could I do?

My friend and I were both strip-searched and thoroughly interrogated. I was scrutinized with the vengeance that might be shown toward someone who was smuggling explosives or drugs into the country. Obviously, what we possessed was very threatening to them! Their anger became more intense with every question.

"What are you intending to do here? Why have you come? Why did you bring these illegal books?"

"Is it wrong?" I asked, trying to be naive.

"Yes! It is wrong to bring Bibles, and you are under arrest!"

The pitch in my voice became higher with every word I spoke.

"But I read in *Soviet Life* magazine and other publications that there is freedom of religion here! So your magazines must tell lies!"

"No! You do not understand. We have freedom, but Bibles are illegal!"

"But Soviet pastors have lectured in America and—"

"We even take Bibles from pastors!"

With my palms sweating and my voice sounding like I was going through my second adolescence, I continued. "So it is illegal to have Bibles?"

"Yes!"

"Is this a new law?"

"No, it is an old law!"

"Then why have Soviet tour guides told us that Bibles are plentiful and there is no religious persecution?"

"No Bibles! Bibles are illegal!"

Not having slept on the flight from Seattle, I had been awake for about thirty-six hours. As the interrogation ground on, I became even more exhausted and at times extremely frightened.

I counted on the scripture that tells us the Holy Spirit will give us the words to say when we are brought before kings and questioned for the sake of Jesus Christ.

Although I was greatly intimidated, knowing God's promises brought me a sense of peace in my heart. It gave me a boldness and a sense that I was in my heavenly Father's hands. The guards could do nothing to me that my heavenly Father would not allow them to do.

I answered their questions with a renewed confidence. I told them the reason I had brought the Bibles was because it was the most important book in my life and it had changed my whole life. Now I felt love for people instead of hatred. I had come to the Soviet Union to deliver the Bread of Life to whoever would take it. I told the guards I was doing this because I loved the Russian people. And then I looked into the eyes of the three Soviet men and said, "I love you too."

In the midst of their questions, anger, and hatred, I sensed a peace that could have only come from God as I answered them honestly.

"Yes, I believe. I believe the Bible is the most special book ever written, and I believe what it teaches." I told them I wanted to share this special book with the Soviet people.

The Soviet guards had power and authority over me. My future was in their hands, yet in a strange way, they were more fearful than I was. They were a part of a system based on fear, hate, and atheism.

After a thorough interrogation, I was asked to sign a paper admitting my guilt to smuggling illegal contraband. When I checked my suitcases, I saw that they had confiscated all the Russian Bibles and Christian booklets I had been carrying. I also noticed they had stolen some of my clothes and money. When I questioned them about the missing things, they responded, "Do you want to make additional trouble?" Knowing I would be in a lot of trouble if I said another word, I silently shook my head.

After our release, my friend Joe and I did not speak on the ride into Leningrad. We were still pretty frightened and didn't know we were free until they took us to a hotel in the city.

As we unpacked and talked through what had just happened to us, we agreed that we had been part of a battle that was bigger than the KGB questioning us. I had sensed an evil about the guards as they had questioned me. I could almost hear the swords of the spiritual warriors clash as I was under attack. The guards had no personal reason to be angry about Bibles. Obviously, they were driven by an unseen force. It was clear—Satan hates the Scriptures. The Bible says he is very deceptive, and he takes on many disguises to accomplish his mission. He comes as a roaring lion, a subtle angel of light, or whatever it takes to accomplish his objective of destroying lives.

There is more to life than meets the eye. The Bible says, "For we are not fighting against people made of flesh and blood, but against persons without bodies—the evil rulers of the unseen world, those mighty satanic beings and great evil princes of darkness who rule this world and against huge numbers of wicked spirits in the spirit world" (Eph. 6:12 TLB).

The anger behind the Soviet government's hatred for the Bible and those who believed in it was obviously a demonic strategy. Thousands of believers were tortured in prisons, and many lost their lives for their beliefs. I believe the time of strict Communist rule and religious suppression was one of the saddest times in history for the people of Eastern Europe and the former Soviet Union. It was an indicator of Satan's anger and an example of what can happen when he uses evil people to carry out his strategy.

We see lives ruined by the many evils of this world such as drug abuse and sexually transmitted diseases, but what we don't see is the rejoicing of the evil army as human life is degraded. We see death all around us in many unnatural forms including hunger, drug overdoses, and abortion; we don't see Satan's forces claiming victory over life itself.

But we are equipped for the battle with Satan and his army. The sixth chapter of Ephesians tells us that God gives us: the belt of truth, the breastplate of God's approval, shoes that are able to speed us on to carry God's good news, the shield of faith to protect us from the darts the evil forces throw at us, the helmet of salvation, and the sword of the Spirit, which is God's Word.

From the battle for the world to the battle for the family to the battle for the soul, the struggle is real; no one has more to lose than Satan.

One giant battle in which Satan was defeated was with a friend of mine from a small town in Iowa. Chuck was addicted to alcohol. After getting drunk one night and being thrown out of a tavern, Chuck crashed his car into a tree. He returned to the tavern where he had been drinking only to find it closed. He smashed the door in and, in a rage, threatened to kill the police officer who came to the scene. Unable to restrain Chuck, the officer enlisted the help of another and followed Chuck home. Using mace, the police were finally able to subdue the wild man and bring him to jail.

Chuck had already lost his job, and his wife was considering divorce. Chuck was losing everything. Yet, he had everything to gain! That night, I had the opportunity to minister to him in jail. At 2:00 A.M. in that jail cell, Chuck asked Jesus Christ to come into his life, and his life was forever changed!

Chuck eventually became an owner of a construction company, and he began to live with the light of Christ shining through him. One day, Chuck was working to finish a job so he could help me drive our truck full of furniture cross-country. Shortly before we were to leave, I received a call that filled me with sorrow. While at work, a 700-pound tile fell and killed Chuck that day. He was only fifty years old. Just before work that morning, he had read John 14:27 where Jesus says, "Peace I leave with you; my peace I give you. I do not give to you as the world gives. Do not let your hearts be troubled and do not be afraid."

Many people who knew Chuck said religion would do him no good. They were right; it wasn't religion but rather his relationship with Jesus Christ that changed his life. Chuck had many friends that came to find hope in Jesus as a result of Chuck's words and life.

Chuck had found peace in that jail cell and discovered what it meant to be free from the things that had once ensnared him. He knew what it meant to be free to really love others as well as himself. Chuck knew Jesus. I struggled with the guilt I felt over Chuck's death. Part of me wrestled with, "If only he hadn't been trying to finish that job so he could help me." And yet I, too, found peace in the promise that Jesus gives in John 14:27—"Peace I leave with you; my peace I give you."

There have been many battles fought throughout history, and many courageous stories have been told about victories over insurmountable odds. In the autumn of 1992, I made my first visit to Volgograd, formerly called Stalingrad, in Russia. It had been the site of a massive battle where the German army lost over two million soldiers, the Russians lost at least a million, and the city had been completely destroyed. Yet, there are many stories of heroism told in this city today. One story I heard on my visit was how fifteen soldiers, holed up in a house, withstood the barrage of several hundred German soldiers for several days.

The city of Leningrad, now renamed St. Petersburg, withstood a German siege for over nine hundred days. Hitler was so confident of victory that he had banquet tickets printed for a victory celebration to be held at the Astoria Hotel banquet hall. Yet even though countless lives were lost to starvation and the effects of war, the city held back the enemy.

I see a similarity in our lives. Sometimes, the battle seems to rage on day after day; it looks like we'll be defeated—but we must recognize the forces behind this battle. As believers in Jesus Christ, we must know the authority that we have. Scripture promises that "the one who is in you is greater than the one who is in the world" (1 John 4:4). If we have Jesus Christ within us, we will have the victory in all battles.

Chapter Five

AGAINST INCREDIBLE ODDS

One of my favorite stories I love to tell is found in the Scriptures. Daniel 3 talks of three courageous young men, possibly teenagers, who went against the crowd and refused to bow to a false god.

Have you ever heard of Shadrach, Meshach, Abednego, and King Nebuchadnezzar? I call them Shad, Meesh, Abad, and Nebacould Sneezer.

King Sneezer built a golden image ninety feet high. He proclaimed to the nation, "Dudes, when you hear the tunes, play kiss the canvas and worship the golden boy!"

Everyone was doing it: governors, advisors, judges, old people, and teenagers. Throughout the day the sounds of horns, pipes, lyres, zithers, harps, bagpipes, and every kind of instrument rang out. People dropped to the ground and worshiped the golden image.

A snitch told Sneezer, "Dude, when the tunes jam, Shad, Meesh, and Abad—they don't kiss the canvas."

The three were brought before Sneezer. Sneezer urged, "Dudes, don't be clunkheads. Everybody is doing it. Don't rock the boat. Dudes, you gotta bow."

They answered, "No way. No can do. We gotta serve God and God alone."

The Sneezer was ticked. "Dudes, if you don't kiss the dust, you're gonna fry in the furnace."

They shrugged, "Whatever."

"Okay you turkeys, you think you're cool. You're gonna be hot stuff when I cook your tails."

Sneezer ordered the clinker boys to stoke up the furnace seven times hotter than usual.

He ordered some jocks, "Cats, glom these three. Bind them with ropes and toss them into the furnace."

The heat was intense. The jocks charcoaled instantly when they tossed the three into the furnace. Shad, Meesh, and Abad's ropes sizzled. They stood up, slapped high fives and said, "This is really hot. Isn't this a gas? We serve an awesome God."

The clinker boys pumped more coal into the fire. The flames leaped high above the furnace.

King Sneezer wiped his nose in disbelief. He leaped from his barbecuing chair.

"Dudes, look! The doo-doo heads standing too close to the furnace fried. Hey, didn't we tie up three? There are four dudes cruisin' in there! The fourth looks like a child of the gods! Whoa! Come out dudes! You serve an awesome God!"

Shad, Meesh, and Abad slapped a few more high fives with their friend and stepped out from the heart of the fire. The magistrates and advisors crowded around to check them out. Their clothes had not been scorched. Their hair wasn't singed. Only the ropes that bound them had burned!

They were able to overcome incredible odds with the fourth person in the fire. That fourth person wants to be in our daily lives. His name is Jesus Christ. He promises to give us strength, comfort, and courage to overcome the odds we face day after day.

Like these Biblical teenagers, a friend of mine took a stand for God. Dave faced a tough situation. He had to make a decision many students have to make daily in their stand for Jesus Christ. He was proud to be a Christian. He wore T-shirts with Christian sayings such as, "Wimp to Warrior for Christ" and "Powered by Jesus."

Dave asked a beautiful young girl to the prom. She was popular, and he was excited when she said yes. A couple of days later, she told him, "I'm embarrassed by your shirts. You're going to have to stop wearing them if you want to take me to the prom."

Dave chose not to compromise his beliefs and his style of witnessing. He made a bold decision. He told her, "This is me, and if you don't want the shirts, you don't want me. So I guess we won't be going to the prom." That's a tough decision for the average Christian. To make those kinds of choices is what it takes to live life on the edge, to be sold out and radical, to have your love for Jesus Christ be number one in your life.

I'm not talking about being a geek for God. I'm talking about making a bold stand. Dave's choice can be an inspiration to many young people. Often, there is a price for standing up for your beliefs. It may not be a popular option, but when we stand firm, some people will respect us for it. Through God's love, you can find confidence in yourself and a growing sense of His purpose in your life.

I, too, have faced situations where I would not have made it through without God's helping hand. I'll never forget one of those times when the odds were against us and all we had to save us was an urgent answer to prayer. We were smuggling Bibles into China. It was in the early 1980s, a very difficult time in China's history. There had been a great purge. Two hundred thousand people had been arrested and, according to some reports, thirty thousand had been executed.

The borders were sealed, and no literature was being allowed in. Some who had brought Bibles in had been stopped, arrested, and even executed.

Our sponsoring organization told us it had been difficult for anyone attempting to take literature into China. We were told they would rather we didn't attempt to do so at that time, but we had come too far to turn back. If we were going to be arrested for taking a little literature into the country, we would just as soon be arrested for taking a lot in. We took all the material they would give us.

"If you make it (How reassuring!), this will be the largest shipment of Scriptures ever brought in by a group of couriers. Pray that you get the red star on your luggage tickets, which means you are okay and you probably won't be checked again."

Like athletes before a big game, we were very nervous the night before. It was the kind of feeling you have when you have worked long and hard to prepare for something that's going to finally happen. We were nervous, but if we were ever ready, it was then.

When our train arrived at the Chinese border, the Hong Kong personnel got off the train, and the People's Republic of China representatives boarded. They asked each of us for passports and visas, making sure they were in order.

They were also checking people's luggage, asking which bag belonged to whom. When they came to our car, they asked for our passports and visas. I was nervous, but I also felt God's peace. I prayed to get the red star on my declaration form and baggage tickets.

None of us received the red star. As the train pulled away from the Hong Kong border, my throat was dry and my hands shook. What would happen when we arrived at the customs office in Canton? It was a long, two-hour ride into Canton. I stared out the window, watching the Chinese countryside streak by. I was thinking about a scripture I had been speaking on in Japan a few days earlier. It was in the sixth chapter of Joshua and spoke about the odds against a man named Joshua.

Joshua was a brave man who was given the charge of bringing God's people into the land that God had promised them, yet they had one problem. There were people already living there who were much better equipped for battle than Joshua and his followers.

The city of Jericho was key to the conquest of the promised land. There was a great wall around the city, with houses and watchtowers built into it, and chariots driving all around it.

The guards in the watchtowers saw a strange sight. Joshua had followed the Lord's command and told seven priests to circle the wall once a day for seven days while blowing horns. Some armed men walked silently before the priests. The priests were followed by the ark of the Lord, which was symbolic of God's presence with the Israelites. The ark was followed by the rear guard.

The procession must have looked pretty harmless to the men in the watchtowers! Imagine what they must have reported to their superiors, "They're just walking around with their religious things, blowing horns! No problem!"

But Joshua and the people followed the Lord's instruction. On the seventh day, they let out a trumpet blast and a shout, and the walls came tumbling down! Jericho now belonged to God's people!

Like Joshua, I had to rely on God to give me the strength to see a way, even through incredible odds such as facing the walls of Jericho. The experience of going into China challenged me to trust the Lord beyond my own strength.

I prayed for God's strength as the train approached Canton. The train slowly pulled into the railway station. We all grabbed our bags, and in a tense quietness, we made our way to the customs hall. Nervously, I looked around to see what was happening. I was one of the first in our group to take my place in the customs line. It seemed some were being let through without having their luggage searched. Still others had their suitcases opened by the guards and the contents were being scrutinized. It was finally my turn. I looked the young Chinese official squarely in the eyes, praying for the courage of Joshua while I answered a couple of routine questions. Within minutes, he nodded for me to pass through. He hadn't even asked me to open my suitcase. I wanted to shout! It was as though the walls of Jericho had fallen! Now my thoughts turned toward the others in our group. I stood silently by the city exit to watch the rest of the group. All but one of us made it through without having to open our suitcases. The last person in our group was being questioned more thoroughly, and they were digging through his handbag. Fourteen of us held our breath. What would happen to our friend? Would we be separated? What would we do if he was sent back? Would they check us when they found his Bibles? We could hear the official questioning him about books.

He simply opened his bag to show the officials two books about China that he had purchased in Hong Kong. It seemed like forever before he was allowed to proceed. When he saw us watching, he gave a big smile like nothing had happened. We had safely brought in a precious shipment of Bibles for our Chinese brothers and sisters in Christ. Our prayer was answered, and now we had to safely deliver the Scriptures to our contacts so they could be given to those believers who did not have Bibles.

Like a good spy novel, we met and exchanged bags with people who were dressed like Hong Kong Chinese and peasant Chinese. Eventually, word got back to us that the mission was accomplished and all the "gold" had arrived. The Bibles had been put into the hands of believers. We had beaten incredible odds; God had been with us in the fire.

Sun, the Chinese national guide who traveled with us in China, was an atheist. He was an intelligent twenty-five-year-old man who spoke five languages fluently, and he used every one of them to tell us he was an atheist. He believed only in himself; but one dark night, he found his way to my hotel room. He was facing some difficult struggles in his life. He said he didn't want to live another day, and the odds were that if he didn't find some answers, he wouldn't. When he came to my hotel room that night in Shanghai, he was so lonely and depressed that he was contemplating suicide. He spilled out his pain for an hour and a half.

I told him I could identify with his feelings of suicide because I had experienced them many times in my teenage years. I shared how Jesus Christ had brought meaning and purpose into my life. He listened attentively as I told him about the life of Jesus and the promise of life with a purpose when committed to living for Christ. He gladly received the Chinese New

Testament and literature on how to become a Christian. Late that evening, he left my room promising to read the books I had given him. That was the last I saw of him for almost thirty-six hours.

I was very concerned about his disappearance and was greatly relieved when he showed up two days later in the hotel restaurant. He approached my friend Scott and me with a question.

"What is the ritual to become a Christian?"

We went to his room with him and explained that there was no ritual; he simply needed to pray, ask God for forgiveness of his sins, and surrender his life to Jesus Christ. He prayed and put his faith in Christ that day.

During the next two weeks, Sun carried his New Testament everywhere. At the conclusion of our tour, he made a farewell speech saying, "Before you came, my heart thought about suicide. Now it thinks about Jesus. It was God's will that you came."

We said good-bye through many tears.

I didn't know if I would ever hear from Sun again, but four years later, a friend I had traveled with called from Canada. He reported that Sun was in Vancouver, British Columbia, attending a university. He was growing in his Christian faith.

He had not dared attend church in China during those four years for fear he would lose his job and opportunity to study in Canada, but he read his Bible every day and prayed without giving up.

"Some days I would sense Jesus standing with me," he said.

He will be going back to China to be an influence for Christ among intellectuals. What an impact his life will have! He won against some pretty tough odds.

More than once I have beaten the odds, but I had a personal fear that was tougher than any border I had faced. For years, I battled a fear of water. Just before I became a Christian, I nearly drowned in a gravel pit. I was drunk, and I took a deep breath, thinking my head was out of the water; it wasn't. Gulp! I wasn't that thirsty! My fear of the water grew over time. While speaking at beach camps, I'd hide in my room during swim time for fear of being thrown in.

We moved to Phoenix, Arizona. It gets a bit hot there in the summer, sometimes up to 115 degrees, occasionally cooling down to 106 degrees. Many houses in Phoenix have swimming pools to beat the heat; I had to conquer my fear. My brother-in-law and a friend worked with me. At first, they would catch me when I jumped in the pool. After a few days, my fear was gone. A month later, I went on a river-rafting trip, and at the end of the trip, I saw some local kids jumping off a thirty-foot bridge. I wondered if I was really over my fear of water. The kids urged me to jump. Thirty feet looks a lot farther from above the raging water than it does from below. Fear gripped me, but after much hesitation, I jumped, screaming the entire way down. I hit the water and swam to the edge of the river. The students who had known me over the years could hardly believe it. They cheered and urged me to jump again. No problem; I climbed the bridge again, stepped off, and ran in place in mid-air as I laughed all the way to the water's surface. Wow! I was over my fear of water— and heights!

We all experience some fear when facing a disaster or something greater than us. This is natural, but knowing Jesus can dispel any of your fears. The Bible says in the last days, people who don't know Jesus will fear so greatly their hearts will fail them.

Recently, I flew out of Oakland, California. A football team was on board. They were loudly bragging about the party they'd been to, and they were still partying. The plane was delayed because it was overweight, but after some of the luggage was unloaded, we took off. About forty-five minutes from Phoenix, the plane nose-dived. Fear was thick on the plane. The macho football players screamed, cried, and clung to one another. What a picture of life with no eternal hope. I'm so thankful for the strength and comfort the Holy Spirit gives us in our times of fear.

Another area in which I have experienced God's strength is in sharing the message of Christ in hostile situations. I was about to speak at a military academy in San Salvador when a young cadet told me, "We learn to hate Christians here. Our instructors say that being a Christian is a sign of weakness, and many of the men are bitter toward anyone who is a believer."

I secretly hoped the engagement would be canceled. I was not looking forward to facing more than one hundred El Salvadoran military men who felt like that! But knowing that this academy recruited only top-quality students and these men could be the future leaders of their country, I realized I had an opportunity few would ever have.

One of the cadets from the academy was excited about my speaking. "I am the only Christian in the academy," he said, "and I'm afraid to let anyone know that I am a Christian."

I walked up the steps of the academy, cleared with the guard, and signed in. As I walked into an open courtyard, I could see the men involved in a drill. The man in front would yell sharply, and the cadets responded in the same sharp voice. It sent chills down my back as I realized I would be speaking to them.

They marched into the building where I was to address them. When my interpreter and host arrived, I walked into the room. The men were all sitting at attention, staring straight ahead. I was introduced and stood to speak.

I looked at the men in front of me. Their cold, stony faces reminded me of the Russian border guards. I tried a few humorous stories, but they didn't crack even a tiny smile. I realized I couldn't rely on my skill, wit, or my own words. I thought, *This opportunity could be a total failure unless God intervenes.* I began to pray inside. Almost in desperation, I asked the Holy Spirit to give me the words and the boldness to speak to these men's hearts.

Soon the words were coming to me in such power that the interpreter could hardly keep up with me. When I started quoting Scripture, I grasped a new sense of the Holy Spirit's anointing. I could see the stony faces growing soft under the impact of God's Word. I spoke for more than forty-five minutes with the strength and authority God had given me.

After the meeting, many of the men came forward to thank me. Once again, the Lord showed me He is always faithful when I choose to be controlled by the Holy Spirit. It doesn't happen without that decision to rely on Him completely and be under His control.

Joshua gave the people of his day a choice: "Choose for yourselves this day whom you will serve...But as for me and my household, we will serve the Lord" (Josh. 24:15).

In Romans, I find another promise from God's Word that has helped me many times. "What, then, shall we say in response to this? If God is for us, who can be against us?" (Rom. 8:31).

I continually strive to have that kind of faith and that kind of love for Christ!

"Who shall separate us from the love of Christ? Shall trouble?" (Rom. 8:35). I've seen people around this world who have been in great trouble and who are facing trying times in their lives, yet it doesn't separate them from their love for Christ.

How about hardship? No, I've been with those who have lost everything and remained dedicated to their faith.

How about persecution? No, I've been with those who showed me blisters and marks where police had beaten the flesh from their bodies. Their only crime was loving Jesus.

Famine? No, I've seen those suffering from famine. I've seen the bellies of little children protruding from malnutrition.

"No, in all these things we are more than conquerors through him who loved us" (Rom. 8:37). We love God more boldly after facing hard times.

"I am convinced that neither death nor life, neither angels nor demons, neither the present nor the future, nor any powers, neither height nor depth, nor anything else in all creation, will be able to separate us from the love of God" (Rom. 8:38–39).

Our call is to love God so boldly that our love for Him is all that matters. This means He must be the top priority in our lives, and we must love Him so deeply that we can trust Him in this way. We can face trials and say, "We are more than conquerors. God is with me. God is faithful. God is working in my life, and He will not abandon me. I love Him so!"

I have experienced times that truly tested my faith. While I was attending Lutheran Bible Institute of Seattle, I was going through some of those difficult times. During one of my low periods, a friend named Grace and I went for a walk through the woods, headed for Puget Sound. As we were going along a wooded trail, we came upon a beautiful little valley with a small creek running through it. We sat for a while to enjoy the scene. We thought of Psalm 48 and started singing it together, "Great is the Lord, and greatly to be praised in the city of our God, in the mountain of his holiness." As we looked at the snowcapped Olympic range, we talked about the beauty of mountaintops. We also talked of spiritual mountaintops.

Then we realized we weren't on a mountaintop but in a valley. So much was growing there that could never survive the mountaintop. There was moss on the rocks, and grass was growing out of fallen logs.

Many plants grow well in valleys. We began to compare mountaintop experiences with some of our valley experiences. We concluded it is easier to praise God on the mountains, but it is in the valleys that we grow. God is present, even in the valley, although the shadows cloud our vision of Him at times.

"Even though I walk through the valley of the *shadow* of death," as David wrote, there is no reason to be sad or afraid. God is ready to meet us and teach us during the valley experience (Ps. 23:4, italics added).

Idi Amin was one of the most cruel dictators the world has ever known. He ruled the African nation of Uganda. Thousands were murdered when he was in power—many were Christians.

Brother Andrew, author of *God's Smuggler*, took Bibles to Amin's soldiers during the height of the reign of terror, and he revealed his Bible-smuggling activities in an interview on national television. When the host commented on the danger of such activities, Brother Andrew responded, "Danger? What is danger? There is only one danger. That is to be out of the will of God. If it is the will of God that I be in Idi Amin's army distributing Bibles, I am as safe there as if I stayed home."

Soviet Communist revolutionary leader Vladimir Lenin said, "You can stop religion and destroy their houses of worship, but it is most difficult to stop the 'belief.' " He named the Christians "Believers." It's our belief, trust, and faith that destroys fear. The Bible tells us, "God has not given us a spirit of fear, but of power and of love and of a sound mind" (2 Tim. 1:7 NKJV).

With Jesus Christ empowering us with the supernatural power of the Holy Spirit, we will overcome the odds of fear, loneliness, and difficult circumstances.

Chapter Six

OVERCOMING STRUGGLES

Dave Dravecky pitched eight innings for the San Francisco Giants, allowing the Cincinnati Reds only four hits. It was a miraculous game because his doctors had said he would never pitch again. During the years of 1988 and 1989, Dave was on an emotional roller coaster few people will ever experience. In June 1988, he was told that he had cancer. More than half of his deltoid muscle (across his left shoulder to the top of the arm) was removed, yet less than ten months later, he was back on the mound. The world applauded him as he gave credit to Jesus Christ.

However, a few days after his incredible win against Cincinnati, he writhed on the ground in pain after throwing a pitch in the game against the Montreal

Expos. He had broken his arm. Millions shared his pain as they watched the replays on television. Those who had rejoiced the week before now held their breath. He had given credit to his Lord when things were going well; what would he say now?

"Where is your Jesus now?" snapped a reporter as Dave got off a plane the next day.

"Jesus never promised comebacks," Dave replied. "He only promised never to leave us."

I met Dave while he was working toward his comeback. His faith in Jesus Christ did not waver during the high moments or the low ones. The following year, Dave had to have his shoulder and arm amputated, yet his faith in Jesus Christ continued to carry him. Dave has become an inspiration to millions of people who didn't even know him before he developed cancer. His struggle has not been wasted. His two books, *Comeback* and *When You Can't Come Back,* have been powerful instruments of inspiration for many. His example and friendship has carried me through some difficult times in my own life.

Another professional athlete with a story of courage is Jim Otto. He was an all-pro center with the Oakland Raiders for sixteen years. Jim's family was poor when he was young. He was accustomed to going to school with holes in his shoes and clothes—before holes were fashionable!

For many years, an anonymous person gave Jim a yearly membership to the YMCA. Although he didn't know the source, year after year he accepted the scholarship and used it as much as possible.

He was told he was too small to play football and that he *probably* wouldn't make it in high school, *never* in college, and *certainly not* in professional football.

But Jim set goals and worked hard. He played with

the Miami Hurricanes before he was drafted by the Raiders. Now he has four Super Bowl rings and numerous awards for his distinguished career.

With all of the hard work, fame, and fortune, Jesus Christ is still the most important person in Jim's life. By the way, after Jim's long career was over, he discovered that it was his pastor who had given him the scholarships! His pastor had seen something in him "that could go either way" and thought the YMCA could help him. Had it not been for that pastor recognizing the potential in him, this all-pro center may have never played football.

Not only athletes struggle through hard times. For example, Tom Cruise seems like a man who has it all: money, looks, and fame. But life hasn't always been so easy for him. In a January 1989 interview in *Parade* magazine, he shared how he, like many teenagers, battled the fear of rejection. He also struggled with the learning disorder of dyslexia which causes letters on a page to appear backwards. Imagine trying to learn to read and write when everything is backwards!

Many teachers didn't understand his problem, so Tom was often put with the "slow learners." Knowing that he wasn't impressing anyone with his brains, he wished he could with his looks, but he was scared to death of being rejected. Tom Cruise didn't think he looked good enough!

Tom Cruise's success has come after much hard work. A movie script is hundreds of pages long, yet he reads them pretty well now. Cruise's looks haven't hurt him, but he knows there is more to life than good looks.

I have also met many young men and women who are not famous but who have also overcome struggles, with God by their side. Kevin Rink died at age sixteen of muscular dystrophy. He was only five or six years old when I became the youth director in his church. Kevin began to lose strength and was confined to a wheelchair, yet he was one of the most inspiring young people I had ever met. Although he could not participate in sports, he had a positive attitude. One time, his brother and I were playing soccer in the backyard while Kevin watched from the sidelines. He cheered, screamed, and got as involved as he could get. When we were done, he exclaimed to his mother, *"We've* been outside playing soccer!" That's the way he saw life. He didn't count on looks or ability for confidence, but he did have a positive self-image. He would look into the mirror, smile, and say, "I'm *so* good-looking!"

When I would stay at his house, I would often be awakened by his moans in the night as he cried in pain for his parents to simply turn him over. Kevin had every right to be angry, bitter, or disappointed with life, yet he was filled with joy. He was a participant in life, not just an observer.

His life made a difference in many other lives. The one thing he wanted people to see was not his disease, not his wheelchair, but Jesus in his life.

Debbie was another teenager whose courage touched my life. Debbie had cystic fibrosis, and she was fourteen when I met her at a camp on Lake Superior. During the sessions, I could hear her coughing. On the second day, she asked if we could talk.

"I probably won't live much longer," she said. She wanted to talk about God and why He allows bad things to happen. She had lost a five-year-old brother to the same disease, and she wanted to know why people who do not care to live are helped, while others who want to live so badly are cut down early in life. I had no answers to these questions, but I shared with her about Jesus' faithfulness during the difficult times. We talked about walking with Jesus. On a rock that overlooked the lake, she prayed that she would live her life for Jesus Christ and would trust Him to walk with her. And yes, she prayed for healing.

That was the beginning of a friendship that would last the rest of her life. She became a student at the Lutheran Bible Institute of Seattle. Because we lived near there she visited frequently, and we shared some special times of growing in our faith. One time, I had told her that God takes the weight of the boulder of our sin and throws it into the *sea of forgetfulness*. As that boulder hits the water and disappears from sight, the sound of "tooosh" can be heard. Debbie was a talented artist, and she painted a rock for me as a reminder of this story of God's forgiveness.

God had taken Debbie's burden of pain and suffering and cast it into that sea, and her complete trust was in Jesus. She still struggled, and she still faced an uncertain future, but she used her talent and lived a very full life. What stands out the most about her life is that, in spite of her life-threatening disease, she always had hope that God was walking with her. She was hopeful that He would heal her; but if not, she knew that the moment she passed from this world, she would have eternal life.

Pneumonia took her life, but she still inspires many people, including me. How different would our lives be if we knew that we just had a year, a month, or a day to live? If we lived life with that kind of urgency what a difference it would make, not only in our own lives, but in the lives of those around us.

When we walk with God, we are not alone. God's Spirit is with us all the way. The role of the Holy Spirit is to bring us into a deeper relationship with Jesus. The Spirit leads us into a deeper understanding of God and gives us the words to pray when we don't even know what to pray for. The Spirit leads us into friendships with other Christians who are able to share our problems and our victories.

I nearly died on one of my trips to China after eating some spoiled food. I was suffering from botulism and was so weak that I could hardly find my way to a public restroom in the factory I was touring. In the country of China, a toilet is simply a hole in the floor, and the public ones are so filthy that it's almost impossible to breathe. I stumbled into one, laid down on the floor, and began vomiting. Slowly, I began losing consciousness. The next thing I remember was a doctor picking me up off the floor and saying that I was dying. I was carried to a bus and brought to the nearest hospital.

When I woke up, I didn't even know I was in China! I looked down at my arm to see an intravenous needle—in my vein! It had been used before! Then I noticed ants in my hospital bed!

I hate needles. I can be very bold when I take Bibles into China and the Soviet Union. I can face interrogation by the KGB. But pull a needle out, and I'll run the other way!

Later I learned that the doctors and nurses had been unable to detect a pulse when I was brought in to the hospital. I was deathly ill, half a world away from home. I struggled to find meaning in the mess in which I found myself. Why would God allow this to happen?

My answer came in the form of two special people—my doctor and a man on our tour by the name of Mr. Wong.

Not long after I regained consciousness, I realized I had not been alone as I had suffered through the night. Mr. Wong was a confirmed atheist who debated the existence of God with me throughout our entire journey. In fact, there were times when he vehemently told me I was a fool for believing in God, but Mr. Wong had been at my bedside throughout the night, placing a cool towel on my forehead to keep my fever down. I was overwhelmed by his love and concern for me. I thanked him for staying with me; I had thought I was going to die.

"Tom, you weren't going to die," said Mr. Wong. "I saw God with you." I didn't ask what he meant. I just know that God's Spirit was with us in that hospital room. Somehow, God had revealed Himself to an atheist through my illness.

The doctor who had saved my life was a very kind and beautiful lady. To be the chief doctor for a foreign patient, she had to have been a privileged person, perhaps even a member of the Communist party. She was very special to me, and I thanked God for her skill and her compassion.

Before leaving the United States on this trip to China, I had been given a beautiful white Chinese Bible. I had been instructed to give it to someone special. I did not know how or if the doctor would receive my gift; but the night before I was released, I prayed and asked that if it was God's will, she would be open to receiving this Bible. The next morning, I was able to tell her this was the most special gift I could give her in return for saving my life. I could sense her gratitude as she gladly accepted the Bible. God had led me to that someone special. God used her to save my life.

Just when it seems that life's final wave is about to crash down on you, God sends help. He uses special people to assist us in overcoming our struggles.

Riding the Waves of Life

Chapter Seven

FROM HURT TO HEALING

One of the keys to riding out life's difficult waves is moving from hurt toward healing. The greatest gift God gives us is the gift of forgiveness. It was one of the first lessons I learned as a new Christian, and it changed my life.

Soon after I had surrendered my life to Christ, I was attending Bible college in Los Angeles. The first weeks of adapting to the Christian life-style were a real struggle. One weekend, I was feeling like a failure because I felt that I could not live up to the expectations of being a Christian. I broke the school rules and went out and bought some marijuana and some liquor and tried to forget my struggles. Some of the students saw me, so it was no surprise when I was called to the president's office. I was filled with anger when I walked into his office. I knew I could be kicked out of school for what I had done, but it no longer seemed to matter. I had given up on trying to live the Christian life.

I could tell by Dr. Force's voice that he wasn't angry with me. He started out by asking me, "You had a difficult weekend, didn't you? Please don't tell me what you did; I don't want to have to dismiss you from school. I have been thinking about you and praying for you all weekend. I knew you must have been struggling."

I nodded in agreement. I couldn't speak. It was so hard to believe what I was hearing. I started to cry because of the love I sensed coming from him.

He continued, "I want you to know that Jesus forgives you, and I forgive you. All I ask is that we pray for each other. I will lay hands on you and pray for you, and then I would like you to lay hands on me and pray for me."

I stopped him, "I can't pray for you; you're the president and a perfect Christian."

I'll never forget his next words. He said, "I'm far from perfect, and it takes the same grace to forgive me as it does you." With that he laid hands on me and prayed for me.

Then it was my turn. I don't remember what I prayed because I was so nervous, but when I stood up and embraced him, I knew I was forgiven. I knew I would never struggle with drugs and alcohol again. It would still take me several years before I was completely convinced of God's unconditional love and His gift of complete forgiveness, but that experience changed my life. I've often wondered what would have happened to my life if Dr. Force had not reached out to me the way he did.

I've often shared this truth with others. One

evening as I was speaking at a church in Texas, a young man named Stanley "just happened" to be walking past. He came in out of curiosity and listened as I spoke on forgiveness. At the close, I asked if any would like to give their life to Jesus Christ and receive His gift of forgiveness. Many people came forward, but I was attracted to this fellow who literally ran down to the center aisle of the church.

"Have you been telling the truth?" he asked.

"Yes," I said.

"You mean God can forgive us for *everything* we've done?"

"Yes."

"You mean even like drugs and hookers?"

I shared that the Bible says that if we confess our sins, God is faithful and just, and will forgive our sins (see 1 John 1:9).

"Well if this is true, then quit talking and start praying!"

He began to repeat a simple prayer, one line at a time, after me. After the third sentence, he began pouring his heart out to God. He went into great detail about how sorry he was for all the things he had done. Having done that, he thanked God for his forgiveness. When he finished praying, he got up smiling, saying, "I am brand-new!"

I have found that art often speaks volumes with one simple picture. One painting that inspires me is a Rembrandt hanging in the Hermitage in St. Petersburg, Russia. It portrays the story of the prodigal son. In this well-known parable (see Luke 15), Jesus tells a story about a son who asks his father for his share of the inheritance, and then goes and blows it all on wine, women, and song. It's also about a father who welcomes this son back with open arms. Rembrandt captures the son in ragged clothes, a sandal lost, weakened and on his knees before his father. The thing you notice about the father is his eyes, which are full of love and tears. For years, the Soviet guides commented that the father was blind. They did not know that the Bible says, "But while he was still a long way off, his father saw him and was filled with compassion for him; he ran to his son, threw his arms around him and kissed him" (v. 20). This story captures the love our heavenly Father has for each one of us. When you fail, remember how our Father feels; remember that He loves us and forgives our sins.

The father in the story did not stop there, nor did the son. "Father, I have been wrong in the sight of heaven and in your eyes. I don't deserve to be called your son anymore."

His father said to the servants, "Hurry, fetch the best clothes." This is what God does for us. He clothes us with the robe of righteousness and heals our hurts with His forgiveness. What a thrill to know that we can stand before God, trusting Him, knowing that we are without condemnation and without guilt. God has clothed us in His best righteous robe, the one that Christ's sacrifice has provided for us. God looks at us and sees us as completely forgiven.

"Put a ring on his finger," the father said to the servants. This was the family signet ring, which showed he was accepted as a full member of the family.

"Put shoes on his feet." Only the wealthy wore shoes. Just as the prodigal son, we are members of God's royal family, and all His wealth is ours.

"Kill the fatted calf." The father gave his best to celebrate the return of his son, the same way our heavenly Father does for us.

"This is my son. He was dead, and now he is alive again. He was lost, and now is found."

I have identified with this story, not just when I first met Jesus, but also when I have been swept under by waves of discouragement.

One of the great privileges of my life was co-speaking with Corrie Ten Boom, author of *The Hiding Place*. She was a woman of great faith who endured many hardships in her long life, including surviving Nazi concentration camps. Corrie Ten Boom knew more about forgiveness than most people. When Corrie was a young woman, a man came into her father's watch shop and begged her for money, saying he needed it so the German Gestapo would release his wife.

Later, the Gestapo arrested Corrie, her elderly father, sister, and other family members. They were taken to a concentration camp in a cattle car. While there, she discovered that the man she had given the money to was the person who had turned her family in. She struggled with her hatred, but eventually she wrote the man a letter and sent him a New Testament.

"You have been terrible. You sent my old father to the concentration camp where he died. My sister, Betsy, was tortured for ten months before she died. We have suffered many terrible things. Now I forgive you. My heavenly Father reminded me of His love and forgiveness as I spotted a raven flying freely high above me as I stood in the freezing cold at roll call one day."

Moved by Corrie's letter, he wrote back, "If you can forgive me and love me after what I did to you and your family, then there must be hope for my life. I have asked this Jesus Christ to forgive me of my terrible sins."

Corrie once visited a prisoner on death row in a South African prison.

"Do you know about Jesus?" she asked.

"Yes, I have asked Him to forgive me."

"Do you know who is responsible for you being in prison?"

"Yes!" he angrily snapped, "and I can tell you the name of every person who betrayed me!"

Sensing his bitterness, Corrie replied, "Oh, I am so sorry. Jesus said, 'If you do not forgive, My Father cannot forgive you.' "

Dmitri had to practice forgiveness more than anyone I've ever met. A few months after he became a Christian, his father, who was a Soviet nuclear physicist, found a package of religious literature in Dmitri's bedroom and turned him in to the secret police. He was put in a psychiatric hospital for examination to see if he was mentally ill for believing in God! He was given mind-altering drugs and electric shock treatments while in the hospital. His parents eventually disowned him because of his faith.

He once told me that he had made a decision to forgive his parents, the KGB, and others who had wronged him. He did not want his anger to destroy him. In spite of all that he has suffered, Dmitri is able to encourage others in their struggles. He has dedicated his life to discipling young Russians in order to reach others with the message of forgiveness. He often takes young Christians to the Russian Art Museum to show them a painting of the early Christians being thrown to the lions in the Coliseum in Rome. "At least we are not being thrown to the lions," he says. "God will not allow us to suffer more than He can give us strength to bear."

Dmitri's life demonstrates that God will indeed give us the strength we need.

Forgiving those who have wronged you is so important. It is a major step to being able to get back up and ride the waves of life. I once asked a group of about six hundred young people how many of them felt bitterness toward their parents or someone else. Fully two thirds of the people there raised their hands!

Bitterness destroys the people who hold it in their hearts and tears at the fabric of relationships in families, friendships, and even in the church. The moment you start hating a person, you become a slave.

I once read the statement, "Bitterness in our spirit is like poison in our body. It will infect our thoughts, emotions, and decisions. Its damaging effects will distort our faces and dissipate our health."

There are even medical side effects to bitterness, including loss of sleep, ulcers, and high blood pressure.

An example of the destruction of bitterness is the story of a fifty-eight-year-old skid row alcoholic named Nels. A friend of mine who had been working with Nels had the opportunity to lead him into a relationship with Jesus.

Not long before his conversion, janitors had taken no less than two huge garbage cans full of empty liquor bottles from Nels's hotel room. I would like to say that Nels's life changed dramatically after his conversion, but there were no signs that anything was different in Nels's life. In fact, the disease of alcoholism had weakened his body to the extent that other diseases had set in, and he was near death.

Finally Nels confessed. He told my friend that when he was eighteen, his brother had impregnated his girlfriend, and he had hated his brother ever since.

"In fact, if he were here now, I would kill him!" Nels shouted.

Nels and my friend prayed that God would give him the desire and the strength to forgive his brother. We do not know what happened to Nels. The last we heard, he had returned to the small midwestern town where his family lived. For all those years, Nels had been a slave to his brother, his bitterness, and his bottle.

It's easy to say, "I won't end up on the street," yet the streets are full of people like Nels—someone's son, someone's brother, someone like us.

The book of Ephesians advises us on how to deal with anger and bitterness. In the fourth chapter, we are told not to let the sun go down on our anger. If you are angry, do not sin by letting it fester and nursing a grudge.

One of the great privileges we have as Christians is to be able to go to those we have wronged and ask them to forgive us. We have no guarantee how they will respond, but our responsibility is to ask for forgiveness when we need it and to forgive others when we are wronged.

A great illustration that has helped me many times to forgive those who have wronged me is a story that Jesus tells us in Matthew 18. The servant owed the king ten thousand talents. When he could not pay, the king ordered that he, his wife, and his children were to be sold. The servant begged for mercy. The king was filled with pity and forgave the servant's debt.

The servant immediately went out and grabbed a person who owed him a fraction of what he had owed to the king. The man begged for mercy, but the servant had him thrown into jail.

The king was enraged when he heard of the injustice. He called the servant before him and said, "You evil-hearted wretch! Here I forgave you all that tremendous debt, just because you asked me to— shouldn't you have mercy on others, just as I had mercy on you?" (Matt. 18:32–33 TLB).

Learning to forgive begins with understanding that we are in need of forgiveness ourselves. First we must understand that God has forgiven us; then we are able to forgive ourselves. Then we can forgive others and seek forgiveness of those we have offended.

Forgiveness sets us free from the grip of bitterness. As we have seen in the stories I have just shared, forgiving other people may set them free; it will surely set us free!

There are some steps we can take to deal with bitterness in our lives. First, we must confess our bitterness to God. If possible, we must go to the person, write a letter, or call to ask forgiveness. Give them a clean record! Then we must look for ways to encourage them, pray for them, and be friendly toward them.

When no bitterness exists between us and others, we are free to focus on Jesus Christ for the purpose of becoming more like Him! To reflect His love, joy, and forgiveness is to enjoy life to its fullest!

The greatest example of forgiveness is the one that Jesus Christ showed us through His life and death.

"Crucify Him! Crucify Him!" Jesus was publicly scorned as the crowds pronounced sentence. A mockery was made of justice as the officials broke countless laws between Jesus' arrest and death.

He was whipped, blindfolded, and shoved by the guards as they challenged Him to guess who it was that was pushing Him. They spat upon Him as they shoved a crown of thorns over His head. The guards stripped Jesus and then gambled for His clothes.

After carrying His own cross through the streets of Jerusalem, He was nailed to it and hung to die between two common criminals.

This was the Son of God. He could have struck these people dead. The Bible tells us that He could have called thousands of angels to rescue Him, but Jesus' response was to pray from the cross, "Father, forgive them, for they do not know what they are doing" (Luke 23:34).

Even in His darkest hour, He thought not of Himself but of His Father's will to use His life for the forgiveness of all sin.

Forgiveness is the key that opens our relationship to God. It is the gift that gives us a new beginning every day. When you forgive others and accept God's gift of forgiveness, you can ride out the wave of condemnation and guilt, knowing you are completely forgiven.

Chapter Eight

LETTING OTHERS IN ON THE NEWS

When we hear the good news of forgiveness and of God's unconditional love, we want to share it with others. I have literally traveled the world to tell people the good news about Jesus Christ. There is no greater thrill than seeing people give their lives to Jesus. Yet, many Christians rarely share the message of God's love with anyone. It is so easy to keep it to ourselves.

If it's easy to be a Christian anywhere, it is in North America. We tend to "party" together as Christians. We attend church or a local youth ministry, where we mix with other Christians. We even adopt our own language, "Christianese." It's easy to get caught in a comfort zone.

I've seen kids from outside the church come into a

youth group. There is no way they will feel welcome if all the Christians belong to little cliques. How tragic if God brings a new person in and no one loves that kid to Jesus. Yet I see the opposite in many churches and Christian groups.

It is easy to love our Christian friends. But God wants us to break that wall of comfort and share His love with others.

I was involved in a ministry in Arizona. We were reaching a lot of kids who had never been to Sunday school or church before.

I would say, "Do you know the story of Daniel in the lion's den?"

They'd say, "We don't know that story."

Then I'd say, "Well, you know David. He took the stones..."

"We don't know about the stones David had," would be their reply.

I learned to tell Bible stories completely, realizing that for many it was the first time they had heard them.

One day we had a guest speaker. I told him, "John, this youth ministry is probably different than any youth ministry you've seen. These are kids who have never gone to church. They're just coming to youth group. Our church is growing by about five hundred to six hundred new members each year, and 72 percent of them have never been to church. We have to explain everything to them.

"We've had people ask, 'When you talk of the Old Testament and the New Testament, does that mean there are two Bibles?' Or when we say John 3:16 they ask, 'What's the guy's name you always say and the two numbers after it?' No idea."

John got up to speak. He smiled and asked, "Aren't you glad you're seated in the heavenlies with Christ?" No idea.

Another line was, "Jesus is coming back for His body."

Ick! It's still here?

Or, "Have you been washed in the blood?"

Gr-o-ss!

Many Christians hope to reach people who do not know God's love, yet they are speaking a language non-Christians cannot understand.

For example, a young person might say, "You have nothing to offer me. I can't relate to that when my parents just got a divorce. Will your message help me if I get pregnant or my boyfriend breaks up with me?"

Sometimes we get so out of touch with the world that we no longer know how to communicate. We get so heaven-minded, we're no earthly good. We get excited about witnessing, then ask, "What'll I say? I'm not familiar with anything they like. I'm not up on sports or the news. What will I talk about?"

There's a world full of people crying and waiting for help. Let's allow God to give us creative ideas for relating. We've been empowered for one reason—to be a witness. Acts 1:8 says, "But you will receive power when the Holy Spirit comes on you; and you will be my witnesses..."

We must think about how we can best reach our world. Our global family consists of many different cultures. Keeping up with the many cultures in America is difficult enough. In our youth culture alone, there are many sub-cultures. We have the "athletes," "punks," "new wavers," "stoners," "GQ guys," "Gucci girls," "poor kids," "rich kids," "skaters," "computer whiz kids," kids of different races, highly motivated kids, abused kids, church kids, and unchurched kids, to name a few of the most common labels placed on today's youth.

Within our adult population, we have baby busters,

baby boomers, middle-agers, and senior citizens. There are no less than sixteen ways *family* is defined in the 1990s, and a different strategy is needed to communicate Jesus' love to each of these groups.

Overseas outreach is an even greater challenge. When I speak in many foreign countries, stories which are relevant to our culture have no meaning to those people. Every time I am in a new country, I ask about the things that I should or should not speak about publicly or privately.

I am allowed to speak about sports in North America, but to talk about soccer in some churches in South America would be strictly forbidden, because it is considered "part of the world." In many countries, the left hand is considered dirty. Knowing that, you would not extend your left hand to greet a person or wave good-bye.

Cultural differences need to be studied in order to effectively present the gospel to the world. A major part of communicating is effectively crossing those cultural barriers. There is a need to observe their life-styles and ask, "How can I touch their world?"

The apostle Paul was one of the most effective communicators of all time. A very learned man, he dealt with most of the major cultures of his day. In 1 Corinthians 9, he shares his wisdom in dealing with people who are different:

> Yet I have freely and happily become a servant of any and all so that I can win them to Christ. When I am with the Jews I seem as one of them so that they will listen to the Gospel and I can win them to Christ. When I am with Gentiles who follow Jewish customs and ceremonies, I don't argue, even though I don't agree, because I want to help them. When with

the heathen I agree with them as much as I can, except of course that I must always do what is right as a Christian. And so, by agreeing, I can win their confidence and help them too. When I am with those whose consciences bother them easily, I don't act as though I know it all and don't say they are foolish; the result is that they are willing to let me help them. Yes, whatever a person is like, I try to find common ground with them so that he will let me tell him about Christ and let Christ save him. I do this to get the Gospel to them and also for the blessing I myself receive when I see them come to Christ" (1 Corinthians 9:19–23 TLB).

This was Paul's strategy. Did he practice what he preached? In Athens, Paul became deeply troubled by all the Greek idols he saw throughout the city; yet, when he addressed the men of Athens, he used those very idols in his illustration.

"Men of Athens! I see that in every way you are very religious. For as I walked around and looked carefully at your objects of worship, I even found an altar with this inscription: TO AN UNKNOWN GOD. Now what you worship as something unknown I am going to proclaim to you" (Acts 17:22–23).

Paul affirmed them for being religious. He did not put the Greeks into a position to defend their gods. He knew that Greeks loved knowledge, and he challenged them with a new thought. He went on to tell the people about the God he knew. Out of that crowd of people, some laughed, others wanted to hear more, and a few believed. We might expect similar results if we follow Paul's example.

I long for the day when you and I, who are filled

with God's Spirit, will be effective witnesses. We are called to be an empowered, loving people to take Christ's message beyond our church walls into a world in need of healing.

"Shouldn't we just leave these people alone?" a pastor asked me when he heard that I had shared my love for Christ in front of a Buddhist temple in China. His argument was that the Buddhist people I had spoken to were sincere; that may very well be. As I have traveled in the Far East, I have met many devoted Buddhists and Hindus. i have also visited one of more than one thousand Moslem mosques in Istanbul. Are they sincere about their religion? Yes! They pray at least five times a day. Are their religions another way to God? It is possible to be sincere about any religion, but it is also possible to be sincerely wrong.

Many of us question our beliefs. We hear many different philosophies and beliefs about God. The New Age movement tells us that God is in us, that we are gods, etc. Could we all be right? Isn't the main point that we are sincere in what we believe? I wish I could say we are all right, but there is only one way to God, and that is through Jesus Christ.

I often wish God would have said, "Just believe in your *own way*. Respect each other and try your best."

There is a major obstacle to this way of thinking; Jesus Christ and who He claimed to be. When examining our faith, we must question His claims. Was Jesus who He claimed to be? Or was He a liar or a lunatic?

If Jesus Christ was just a prophet or a good moral teacher, He surely wouldn't claim to be someone He was not. He surely would not lie and deceive his friends and followers. Listen to His claims.

In John 14:6, Jesus says, "I am the way and the truth and the life. No one comes to the Father except through me."

When Jesus asked His followers, "Who do the crowds say I am?" they answered, "Some say John the Baptist; others say Elijah; and still others, that one of the prophets of long ago has come back to life." But when He asked "Who do you say I am?", Peter boldly answered, "The Christ of God!" (Luke 9:18–20).

Jesus claimed to be the Messiah, God in flesh. There were no less than sixty major prophecies pointing to the birth, death, and resurrection of Christ. All of them were fulfilled.

Most of Jesus' disciples died martyrs' deaths because they had faith in Him. If anyone would have known Jesus' resurrection to be a lie, wouldn't it have been those closest to Him? Would anyone die for a lie?

Jesus was crucified on the charge of blasphemy. He had claimed to be God. He also said, "I am the way and the truth and the life. No one comes to the Father except through me" (John 14:6).

Jesus made hundreds of claims we must consider. Those claims have been argued and dissected for two thousand years. Yet today, with our technology and knowledge, there is more evidence available to us which supports the Bible and the claims of Christ than there has been at any other time. Many of the best books supporting the claims of Christ have been written by authors who originally set out to disprove His claims.

In Kiev, Ukraine, I discovered that even college English professors like to practice their English with Americans. One professor had picked up my friend and me while we were hitchhiking. We asked whether we could speak to one of his classes. He said that would be impossible; relations between our two countries were strained at the time. The Americans had just boycotted the Olympics in response to the Soviet invasion of Afghanistan.

After thinking it over, the professor did invite us to attend a class, but he cautioned us to be very careful. We made sure not to wear blue jeans so we would fit in with the college students.

It was a thrill when we thought we were going there to observe, but what a surprise when he introduced us to the class as guest speakers for the day! He invited us to talk about anything we wanted. My friend, who has a degree in Russian history, started by speaking on that subject. Eventually, we changed the topic to God. The students laughed.

"It's just a fairy tale," one said.

"Only the simple believe that," said another.

"The Bible is just a fairy tale book," repeated another student.

"But if it's just a fairy tale book," I asked, "then why were we arrested at your border ten days ago for bringing Bibles into your country? I challenge you. The government is hiding something from you. If these are worthless books, why would they go to all the effort of keeping them from you? That book has stood the test of time, and I challenge you to try to get hold of a copy and read what's in there."

The mood seemed to change from one of mockery to curiosity. They asked many questions, and we freely answered. The professor invited us to his afternoon class.

After lunch, the professor learned that all the conversations in the cafeteria had been about our visit to his class, and the KGB was now looking for us. We were disappointed that we could not go back for the afternoon class, but the message of God's love was spreading throughout the university.

Difficult questions challenge us to study more, to investigate the evidence. However, we don't have to know all the answers before we start witnessing to others.

Biyoun, a waitress in Hangchow, China, responded to the good news of Jesus in much the same way Sun had. Friends and I had given her some literature during a previous visit, and when we visited her again a year later, Biyoun joyously greeted us. We asked about the books we had given her, and she lit up even more.

"I read them. I asked Jesus to be my Lord and Savior, then I gave them to my friends so they, too, could know Jesus. Do you have any more?" She was sharing her new faith from the very beginning.

Sometimes we are hesitant because we are afraid, and it's easier to stay in our comfort zones. I met some young believers in Irian Jaya (in Indonesia) who challenged me by their lives to live beyond my comfort zone. I went with friends into a primitive jungle area to visit a young couple and their child who were living among nomadic tribes. This tribe is just one of approximately one thousand believed to be living in this particular area. The young couple were there to learn the language so that the Scriptures could be translated into the language of the tribe.

This particular tribe is known for their head-hunting and cannibalism. While on our six-hour journey up the river, we met the young family going the other way. They were headed back to the mission outpost where we had been staying because they had been attacked by the tribe—they were fleeing for their lives!

One of the missionaries I was traveling with was in charge of the mission and wanted to investigate the situation. Feelings of excitement and fear gradually grew into terror as we drew closer to the tribe; I did not know what to expect.

The women ran to the river shore and tried to wave us off; we were not welcome visitors. A few minutes after we arrived, the men began to appear, coming out of the jungle and down the river. They, too, were angry and yelled at us.

After convincing them that we meant them no harm, we offered to exchange chewing gum and food supplies we had brought for some of their weapons—spears, bows, and arrows. Then we were able to spend some time communicating with them, and I was thrilled to be able to videotape a portion of our time with them. While we were still not sure what had caused the problem with the missionary family, the senior missionary was able to understand that the people did appreciate what the young family was doing, and they did want them back.

It took us five hours to return to the missionary outpost. The meal of rice, beans, fried bananas, and ground meat (we didn't dare ask what it was) wrapped in a banana leaf tasted as good as anything I have ever eaten.

After all the events of the day, the thing that struck me the most was the young believers with their family, being sent from this outpost to the tribes. *Their* young children were suffering from malnutrition, parasites, and malaria; *their* children's eyes were filming over because of a lack of vitamin A. What servants' hearts!

I lay on my cot under a piece of steel nailed to a tree, hearing the children crying through the night. The young student missionaries were preparing to go back to the tribe they had served for the past nine months. Their example of servanthood pushed me beyond my comfort zone. I was greatly challenged to pray for an attitude like theirs, which would allow me to go and reach out to people who have never had the chance to hear about God's great love.

There is a great Old Testament story that can help reawaken us to the responsibility we have to the people who still haven't heard the gospel. Second Kings 7 tells us of an event that takes place around 845 B.C. during the time of Elisha, the prophet. The Syrians had completely surrounded and sealed off the city of Samaria. Food was terribly scarce, so extremely high prices were required for small amounts of food. People were starving to death daily. Hope was lost for this city; soon they would need to surrender to the enemy.

There were four lepers sitting at their place outside the city gates. Facing imminent death, they decided to approach the enemy's camp. What they found was that the enemy had run because the Lord had "made the whole Syrian army hear the clatter of speeding chariots and a loud galloping of horses and the sounds of a great army approaching" (2 Kings 7:6 TLB). Fearing that the Israelites had hired soldiers from other countries, the Arameans fled.

When the four lepers got to the camp, they found food and silver. The Bible says they ate until they could hardly move. They had to lean up against a tree. There was more than enough for the four of them, and no one else knew that the Arameans were gone! They could have hidden many of the riches and hoarded everything for themselves. But they sensed the tug of responsibility to others. They said, "This isn't right. This is wonderful news, and we aren't sharing it with anyone. Even if we wait until morning, some terrible calamity will certainly fall upon us; come on, let's go back and tell the people at the palace" (v. 9 TLB).

We in North America are like the lepers in that camp. We have more than enough material resources and Christian resources for growth. We have a decision to make. Will we selfishly say, "I deserve what I have—it's mine," or will we respond, "This is the day of good news. I must share it with others"?

A great example of someone who felt that urgency to share the good news of Christ was the apostle Paul who said, "For just preaching the Gospel isn't any special credit to me—I couldn't keep from preaching it if I wanted to. I would be utterly miserable. Woe unto me if I don't" (1 Cor. 9:16 TLB).

Sometimes there is a great risk in sharing the good news. Paul knew what it meant to live beyond the comfort zone. In Paul's time, there was a Roman law prohibiting a person from being whipped with forty lashes. Paul was whipped with thirty-nine lashes five separate times. He was beaten with rods three times and stoned once. He was shipwrecked three times, spent twenty-four hours on the open sea, and lived in constant danger from rivers, bandits, his own people, and pagans.

Paul knew sleepless nights, exhaustion, hunger, thirst, cold, and exposure. Christianity is not for wimps! The Christian life is an exciting, challenging way of life.

Chapter Nine

LIVING THE LIFE OF COMPASSION

One cold winter night in St. Petersburg, Russia, I visited a children's hospital with several pastors from our church in Phoenix, Arizona. Galena, the head doctor, showed us through her hospital. There were over 120 babies in this hospital, but the staff had few medical supplies. They were reusing syringes and bandages, and their primitive incubators had been built in the 1930s. They did, however, have two brand-new incubators. These had been given to them by a Finnish Evangelist, Kalevi Leittinen, when he had held a Christian meeting in the city. Galena had given her life to Jesus Christ as a result of that gift to her hospital. She said that she had no interest in God before Kalevi showed that great act of love.

After talking with Doctor Galena, I promised to

return with a group in the summer to bring them more medical supplies. She gave us a list of the supplies they needed most.

Six months later, on a warm June day, my wife, Diane, and I walked into her office. She had a great look of surprise, and she smiled at us.

Through Lena, our interpreter, she told us about a meeting held with her staff the day before.

"Yesterday, we were talking about you and had decided that you were not going to return to our hospital. We had given up hope. Now, here you are today."

I excitedly responded, "I am very sorry I worried you. In two days, our team will deliver sixteen duffel bags full of medicine and medical supplies. We have brought many things that were on your list, including bandages, antibiotics, and seven thousand syringes."

One of the doctors standing in the office began wiping tears from her eyes. Galena turned to us and explained, "This would be her greatest dream, to see these syringes."

As promised, two days later fourteen teenagers and six adults delivered the medicine to the hospital. What a thrill it was to watch the doctors open each of the boxes. I don't think Diane and I have ever been hugged and kissed more, and I was so proud that American teenagers had been involved in collecting and delivering this medical relief.

I have lead youth teams all over the world, and I've seen the impact these mission trips make on their lives. I am convinced that one of the quickest ways to help us get up on the wave again after we've been pounded down by our own problems is to reach out in compassion and help someone in need.

We are called to reach out in Christ's love. I was reminded of this when I spoke at a camp run by a Minneapolis police officer.

"You're a liar," the ninety-five-pound, nineteen-year-old said as she looked at me with eyes of steel.

Melody was involved in drugs, alcohol, prostitution, and witchcraft, and she was responding to a message I had just delivered on Christ's love and forgiveness. I had stressed, "It's so great to be a Christian because Christians love each other. We're so full of love for others."

Melody and her friend challenged me, so I asked her to explain.

"You're telling us about how God loves us. God doesn't love us. And another thing, you say how loving Christians are? I've never been told by a Christian that I'm loved. I've only been told by Christians how awful I am and what's going to happen to me."

Immediately I wanted to blame other Christians. I wanted to say, "Well, you know those older Christians. They get that way. They're not as understanding as we younger ones." But as I was about to say that, the Spirit of God spoke to me. "She's talking to *you*."

At once, I saw that I'd become a prideful speaker, a step above those around me. The Spirit of God broke me. I knew He had clearly called me to love young people, and He had plainly told me to love kids unconditionally. It doesn't matter how they look, dress, wear their hair, talk, or what they do; I'm to love them as they are, as Jesus loves them.

I looked at Melody and her friend. With a heavy heart I said, "I'm sorry. But I'm one of those Christians who has felt that I'm better than you are." I started crying, "I'm so sorry. I want you to know Jesus Christ loves you."

"Prove it," she demanded.

"The best I can do is tell you a story from the Bible." I told of the woman caught in adultery. The religious people brought her, naked, and threw her at

Jesus' feet. Jesus said, "If any one of you is without sin, let him be the first to throw a stone at her" (John 8:7). He bent down and began writing in the sand. Some say He listed the sins of the people. One by one the people slipped away. Jesus looked up and asked, "Where are your accusers?"

She said, "They've gone."

Jesus said, "Neither do I condemn you. Go and sin no more."

Melody and her friend Shawna began to cry. Melody asked, "You mean Jesus will forgive me and give me a new start, just like He did to that girl?"

"Yes, He will," I answered.

We knelt in the dirt road. Shawna and Melody invited Jesus into their lives.

Ten years later, I was speaking at a church in Minneapolis. Afterward, a woman approached me at the altar. She said, "I don't think you'll remember me, but ten years ago, we knelt and prayed together."

"Melody?"

"How did you remember my name?"

"I've been praying for you. I've told your story many times."

She smiled. "I had to come and tell you I've been walking with Jesus since that day. I'm in Bible college now, and I'm going into the ministry to help other people like me."

I told her, "God used you in my life to teach me not to prejudge anyone He brings to me. You were my reminder that He called me not to judge but to love."

God continues to shower us with His love and His faithfulness. Diane and I had the opportunity to experience being loved by a special people in South Africa. I had been invited to speak in a Muslim area, and the meetings attracted people of many different races. While there, we received special permission to go into a black township to preach to the Xlohsa tribe. The morning service was held in a school building, and although the building was not large, it was filled to capacity. I had to stand with my back against the wall to speak.

The tribal language is a series of clicking sounds. I could only know that the interpreter was repeating what I was saying by the response of the people. The music during the worship was so exuberant that they danced as they sang, and the building nearly shook. The children all sat together for the two-and-a-half-hour service. Typically, the sermon lasts about one-and-a-half hours; if a sermon is much shorter, the people think you don't know very much!

At the conclusion of my talk, one of the leaders announced that they would take an offering for me. They began to dance again as music played. There was a small plate on a table in front of me, and the people would dance their way up to the plate to give something from what little they had.

After the offering, a bundled-up package was thrown from one person to another around the room. People smiled and laughed as they caught it and threw it back and forth. Finally the package landed on the table in front of us. One of the leaders opened it, looked at us, and smiled. It was filled with gifts for us: an ebony elephant, beads, and a blanket.

The leader wrapped the blanket around us and said, "To the African, the blanket is everything. It is a shelter in the storm. It is warmth. It is protection from the wind. It carries our babies. You have been like a blanket to us. You have warmed our hearts."

After the service, there were many warm embraces and a great celebration. One divorced couple there had been reunited. They invited us to be honored guests as they celebrated their new life together. We drove through the countryside dotted by government-built brick houses with corrugated steel roofs. As we arrived at the party for this couple, we saw the skins of the sheep that had been slaughtered for the feast. There was a table heaped with fruit, vegetables, and different dishes. We were seated with the bride, groom, and family. They piled the food on our plates, and after the meal, there was more singing and dancing. I have rarely met a people more filled with love!

I especially enjoy speaking to people who have never heard even the name of Jesus. Their curiosity and openness is refreshing in a world where Christianity has often been abused and has gained a terrible reputation.

On our first trip to China, Diane and I went to Shanghai. One evening, as we walked through a park, two boys stopped us and asked if they could practice their English with us. Within a few moments, there was quite a crowd of young people around us. In fact, they were actually standing in the street, blocking traffic! I believe that God leads us and watches our steps, bringing people across our path at the right time. This was one of those times; there was a young man in the crowd who was an interpreter. He said, "You speak too fast. If you slow down, I will translate for you."

Meanwhile, the others were putting Christian literature into their pockets as quickly as we could hand it out. The crowd was so large that my wife and I had to split up.

Everything I said would be interpreted, but I knew I had only two or three minutes to say it before the police would come! I told the story of Jesus in the most simple way I could.

"Two thousand years ago, there was a man named Jesus. He was born in the country of Israel. He did all kinds of incredible miracles. He healed the sick. He even raised the dead."

It was wonderful to see the looks of interest and amazement on the students' faces as the interpreter relayed my message to them.

"He claimed to be God's Son." I continued, "Then they murdered Him on the cross, but He rose from the dead. If you put your trust in Him, He will forgive all of your sins and give you eternal life in heaven."

I noticed that a couple of people in the back were getting nervous, so I called to Diane, "It's time to leave!"

As we turned to go, the interpreter grabbed my arm and said, "You forgot to tell us what heaven is."

After I tried to briefly explain what heaven would be like, he asked, "Could you come back to China and tell all of our young people about this Jesus Christ?"

If ever I heard a call, it was then. I knew I had to come back, and I promised I would. Now, every time I go back, I remember that young man and how God used him to call me.

During another trip to China with my pastors, we asked our guide, Mr. Wu, to take us to a church. Mr. Wu translated the Bible stories for us—Daniel in the lion's den, the three young men in the fiery furnace, and David and Goliath.

Afterward Mr. Wu said, "These are the greatest stories I have ever heard. I must tell my child; he will enjoy these stories!"

We told him that these were not just stories, they were true; these things really happened.

He was amazed. Because he was an English teacher for other Chinese who were learning to be tour guides, he decided that he would use these stories to teach his students. We were able to give him a Bible and other literature that explained the stories more fully, and after he read them, we spent time answering his questions. It is such a privilege and a challenge to bring Bibles and Christian literature into China.

I thought back to my first trip to China. I hadn't been sure what to expect. I had wondered whether I would fall in love with the Chinese as I had the Soviet people.

I remember writing in large letters in my journal, *"Lord, fill my heart with Your love for the Chinese people."*

A few days later, Diane and I were in a rural area, handing out balloons and booklets to the children. Diane was teaching "patty cake" to some children while other children and I were playing with balloons. The children were dressed in rags and covered with dirt. As I admired these beautiful children, my prayer was answered. I was overwhelmed with love, and I began to weep. I loved them so much that I almost felt I knew their individual names. I was seeing them as our heavenly Father sees them, as very special, individual people. They need to hear about Jesus, and they may never hear unless we, and others like us, continue to travel into China.

The more I travel and share and meet people around the world, the more I am challenged to have the attitude of being a servant. I have stayed in homes throughout the world where people have slept on the floor so I could have a bed. I have eaten incredible meals where I know the people stood in line to buy the food. I have a difficult time finding the words to describe these people who have risen above their own problems to shower love on others.

A scripture that I often come back to is, "So then, men ought to regard us as servants of Christ and as those entrusted with the secret things of God. Now it is required that those who have been given a trust must prove faithful" (1 Cor. 4:1–2).

Under-rowers were called servants, and they sat on a narrow bench at the bottom of the ship. The ship's power was in the oars. The under-rower's job was to pull on the oars when the order was given. These oarsmen didn't say, "I'm going to pull the ship this way," or "I'm going off to sea now." They listened for the order from the upper deck where the captain stood.

The Bible tells us that if we are disciples of Christ, we will obey His commandments. To surrender to His will is to say, "I don't want my will; I want the will of the Lord. I want to do what He wants me to do."

Sometimes we rebel at the thought of being servants. We say, "I want to call the shots. I'll go to church and I'll talk about God, but I don't know about surrendering and telling God that I'll do anything. He might send me to Zimbabwe."

The more we surrender to Christ, and the more we give to Him, the more He gives back. God is not waiting for us to give in so He can say, "Okay, where can I send this person—somewhere I know he'll hate? What can I make her do that I know will make her miserable?"

God isn't like that. He gives us the desires of our heart. He gives us tremendous joy as we serve Him.

When we surrender to Christ as His servant, we develop an attitude toward others that exemplifies servanthood. We begin to say, "I am here to serve people. I am here to serve the cause of Christ."

The apostle Paul tells us:

Do nothing out of selfish ambition or vain conceit, but in humility consider others better than yourselves. Each of you should look not only to your own interests, but also to the interests of others. Your attitude should be the same as that of Christ Jesus: Who, being in very nature God, did not consider equality with God something to be grasped, but made himself nothing, taking the very nature of a servant, being made in human likeness. And being found in appearance as a man, he humbled himself and became obedient to death—even death on a cross! Therefore God exalted him to the highest place... (Phil. 2:3–9).

I want to have the attitude of Christ. I have often prayed, "Lord, I don't ever want to think I'm above people. I don't ever want to get into a protected ivory tower as a Christian, looking judgmentally at people and isolating myself from their needs."

I've been exposed to people around the world enduring persecution, poverty, and famine. I believe God has allowed me to see them for a reason; as we serve God, we need to hold an attitude of servanthood. The world can't turn away from it.

The Bible says that in the last days, hearts will grow cold; in the last days, people will be lovers of self and lovers of pleasure rather than lovers of God. Young people are suffering from these attitudes today. They are deeply hurting and are crying out for help.

"Whoever can be trusted with very little can also be trusted with much, and whoever is dishonest with very little will also be dishonest with much" (Luke 16:10).

Many times I'm motivated by wrong desires; then I need to come back to God and say, "All I want to be is faithful—faithful to what You call me to do, faithful to reach those You desire me to reach. Fill me with a compassion for others."

When you are involved in helping others and showing compassion, it is very hard to get knocked off the crest of a wave.

Chapter Ten

FILLED WITH HOPE

My major desire as I write this book is that when you finish reading it, you will be filled with hope—hope that will help you face today and tomorrow.

If my college president gave me one more chance, my father must have given me a thousand. If it were not for Dad's tender love and compassion when everyone else, including me, had given up on me, I'm not sure I would be a Christian today.

When Dad died in 1985, I grieved deeply; but at the same time I had a sense of joy and hope, not because he was gone but because I knew him so well.

Romans 15 tells us that "For everything that was written in the past was written to teach us, so that through endurance and the encouragement of the Scriptures we might have hope" (v. 4).

The kind of hope the Scriptures talk about is more than wishful thinking; hope that is rooted in faith gives us conviction; it gives us something to live for and something to die for. My dad had hope for himself, and he had hope for me when I had none.

Romans 5:1–5 says,

Therefore, since we have been *justified through faith*, we have *peace* with God through our Lord Jesus Christ, through whom we have gained access by faith into this *grace* in which we now stand. And we rejoice in the hope of the glory of God. Not only so, but we also *rejoice in our sufferings*, because we know that suffering produces perseverance, perseverance, character; and character, hope. And hope does not disappoint us...

The words of these verses encompass the message of this book.

Justified by faith—There is nothing we can do to earn God's love or favor. When we put our trust in Jesus Christ, we have the joy of a new beginning.

Peace—We might try to find peace in many ways and in many places, but only through Jesus Christ can we find peace with God, resulting in peace with ourselves and others.

Grace—We have been given the free gift of God's love. That gift may be free, but it's not cheap. Christ has paid the price for us. Grace is God's Riches At Christ's Expense.

Rejoice in sufferings, which bring hope—Remember, this was written to believers in Rome who seemed to have no reason for hope. Believers were being killed, yet Paul is talking about rejoicing. Faith is not just pie-in-the-sky escapist thinking; rather, faith is being able to look beyond the present circumstances, no matter how desperate they may seem, to the promises of Jesus Christ.

Filled with Hope

The first Christians in Rome suffered greatly. Some were tarred and lit as torches, and others were thrown to the lions; while still others endured various forms of torture. It was to these believers Paul wrote, "I consider that our present sufferings are not worth comparing with the glory that will be revealed in us" (Rom. 8:18). Paul adds in verse 26, "the Spirit helps us in our weakness."

God doesn't just say, "Okay, now you know Me, just go out there and try your best! Try it and see if you make it. I hope you survive!" He promises to help us in our weakness.

In 1987, we began to catch a glimmer of hope for new freedoms in Russia. By 1989, when Diane and I were visiting the Soviet Union, changes were starting to take place. We met with Valari, Volodya, and several others we knew, and they introduced us to an eighteen-year-old girl named Anastasia. She was a very intelligent university student who spoke several languages and was knowledgeable about art and history. She was especially fascinated with American Indians and had studied about them. She had also studied the Koran, Buddah, and the Bible. As a new Christian she had many questions about Jesus and wanted to know if He really is the only way to God. During the several days we spent with her, she took us to museums and showed us parts of Leningrad the average visitor never gets to see.

One night we were walking on Nefsky Prospect, the major street in Leningrad. We came to a place I had seen many times. It was the Cathedral of Our Lady of Kazan. The beautiful cathedral had been closed as a place of worship for decades and was the museum of atheism. It lies on a beautiful square where many Christians have been murdered, arrested, and beaten for speaking their beliefs.

This night was different. Groups of people stood throughout the square, and as we listened in, we heard some talking about politics, but most were talking about faith in Christ. I stood on the steps of this museum of atheism and talked with Anastasia. I tried to explain why I believe that Jesus Christ is the only way to God; we have to accept Him as the Son of God or reject Him as a liar or a madman.

Standing there, freely speaking about Jesus Christ, was a dream come true. The oppression was finally lifting from Eastern Europe and the Soviet Union.

Isn't it ironic that those who grow up in the freedom of hearing about God have little interest, but those who have grown up in atheism have a deep hunger? There was a sense of hope for freedom of expression in the air. Little did we know how quickly communism would fall, and soon there would be freedom like we'd never dreamed possible.

There are so many countries that continue to need our prayers. A few years ago, *Time* magazine called Uganda "The Killings Fields of Africa." Hundreds of thousands of people (including Christians, professional people such as lawyers and teachers, and wealthy people) have been killed there over the last two decades because they were perceived as a threat by a paranoid dictator.

Although the dictator Idi Amin is gone, disturbing stories continue to this day. Not long ago, I heard the beautiful voices of the Children's African Choir. Many of them were Ugandan children, orphans of martyred parents who had been killed because of their faith. As the children marched down the aisle of our church, they exuberantly sang "On the King's Highway."

One young boy told the story of soldiers coming to his home and shooting his father in front of the family. Yet these boys and girls had a contagious joy in serving Jesus. They were being ambassadors of encouragement to American Christians who, in comparison, know little or nothing about suffering.

"The blood of the martyrs is the seed of the church," said the choir director. Throughout history, that has been the case. The children of those who have suffered the most have emerged with a great trust for God and are an encouragement to people who have suffered little. These children were a great inspiration to many of us; they represent hope out of tragedy.

> Dear friends, do not be surprised at the painful trial you are suffering, as though something strange were happening to you. But rejoice that you participate in the sufferings of Christ, so that you may be overjoyed when his glory is revealed. If you are insulted because of the name of Christ, you are blessed, for the Spirit of glory and of God rests on you. If you suffer, it should not be as a murderer or thief or any other kind of criminal, or even as a meddler. However, if you suffer as a Christian, do not be ashamed, but praise God that you bear that name (1 Pet. 4:12–16).

A dear friend, Pastor Kallestad Senior (as we lovingly called him), spent the last years of his life ministering to the sick and welcoming new members into our church. Those were, perhaps, the most fruitful years of his ministry. Until his dying day, he was motivated by the desire to see people of all ages know Jesus Christ.

One day he asked me if I had any literature he could share with a Jewish woman he had come to know. Although he was very ill, he was still concerned for others. Later that same day, I received a call and was asked to come and pray for him. A group of us gathered, and he asked us to pray that he would either be healed or that God would take him home. When we finished, he asked whether God's spirit had spoken to any of us concerning him.

I told him that he had always been a great example to me. I saw in him a hope-filled life, full of love for God and others. I told him that the Lord may take him home, perhaps in a few hours, but with the hope we share, there was nothing to fear.

I asked him to pray for us. He laid his hands on each of us and prayed that we would always remain faithful, and that we would never stray from the desire to introduce others to Jesus. He prayed that we would be bold, never ashamed of our faith, and that we would always stand for the gospel.

As I said good-bye to Pastor Senior that day, I had a sense that it would be the last time I saw him. It was.

Later that day, I had the opportunity to share my faith with a neighbor I had never been able to share with before. I believe that was a direct answer to Pastor Kallestad Senior's prayer.

There is a great symbol of hope at the South Korean/North Korean border. The Demilitarized Zone separating these two countries has been home to an ominous tension since the early 1950s. War has been a constant threat with 1.5 million troops lining the border. Yet, for the past forty years, there is a train that sits at the end of the track, poised and waiting for the day it will freely roll north once again. The sign near the train states, "We hope that someday this train that has been stopped by force will again carry passengers freely to the North and to the South."

Living life with hope is often compared to running a race. I enjoy running and have logged many miles running throughout the world. One of my favorite running experiences happened in Africa.

Imagine seeing two guys running through *your* village at daybreak! I had talked a missionary friend into going with me, and although he had never jogged and didn't know what the people of the village would think, he decided to be brave. As we wound through the village, the people were starting their fires to cook breakfast. Children were getting ready to go to school, and some of the villagers were still sleeping.

Shouts went up! What could be wrong? Women came out to the front of their thatch huts, wondering "Where are they going? What is the matter? What is wrong?" Little children ran beside us. We ran through the village, turned around and ran back. How ridiculous!

"They didn't go anywhere!" the villagers shouted. To run without a purpose made no sense at all. To see us sweating and breathing hard was very comical. The children laughed and mocked our hard breathing as they ran with us.

My missionary friend said we'd be the topic of discussion at the campfire that night! Later that day, I spoke at an institute similar to a junior-senior high school. I addressed many important issues, including our need for God. When I opened the class up for questions, I was immediately asked "Why were you running through our village this morning?"

They could not understand that I needed to run to stay in shape and to have energy. They live for survival; the thought of running to lose weight doesn't enter their minds! In fact, many of them are very hungry. I learned later the Swahili word often used for "white man" in that country literally means "man who runs in circles." How fitting for us to be running in circles in their village, causing such an uproar! In their society, what I was doing looked very stupid!

Running can be physically and mentally challenging. Sometimes it helps to have someone run with me. The other person helps me to keep pace and encourages me to keep running when I feel like giving up. While running alone up a long hill, I am sometimes tempted to give up, but there is something that keeps me going. Maybe it's my heart, or my legs, or my mind. Whatever it is, it says, "You can do it! Keep going!" It is hope in reaching a goal that keeps me going. I run to maintain energy as well as for the enjoyment, but others run to maintain physical stamina that enables them to compete in athletic events, where the goal is to win a gold medal.

My nephew Dan and I attended twelve events at the twenty-fourth Olympiad in Seoul, Korea. To scream, wave an American flag, and chant "U.S.A.!" was awesome. We watched in great anticipation as the finest athletes from 160 nations competed for the utmost prize—an Olympic Gold Medal.

Thousands of people from 160 nations, together in peace. It only lasts for a moment; the games are over too soon, and many experience the emptiness of failure.

Who will ever forget the despair of the Korean boxer who sat alone in the ring for seven minutes after losing a bout? Then there was the devastation of the American boxer who, after years of training, missed the event because his trainer misread the schedule.

I am amazed at the number of years the athletes spend training for a few seconds or minutes of competition. The hope of winning the gold medal pushes them to persevere. It is much the same in the Christian life.

In 1 Corinthians 9:24–27 Paul cheers us on to focus on the ultimate goal of eternal life.

In a race, everyone runs but only one person gets first prize. So run your race to win. To win the contest you must deny yourselves many things that would keep you from doing your best. An athlete goes to all this trouble just to win a blue ribbon or a silver cup, but we do it for a heavenly reward that never disappears. So I run straight to the goal with purpose in every step. I fight to win. I'm not just shadow-boxing or playing around. Like an athlete I punish my body, treating it roughly, training it to do what it should, not what it wants to. Otherwise I fear that after enlisting others for the race, I myself might be declared unfit and ordered to stand aside (TLB).

Paul tells us not to just run the race of life but to run to win. Serious competitors in an athletic event go into extensive training, giving up that which would hinder them. We're encouraged to battle against whatever takes us away from our relationship with Jesus Christ. An athlete takes tremendous pains for a fading crown of leaves or a medal. Our contest is for a crown that will not fade or tarnish—eternal life. What can be compared with the value of eternal life?

Paul says, "I run straight to the goal with purpose in every step."

God's desire for us is that we might live a life filled with purpose and direction. If we aren't doing that, we need to examine our goals. Are they self-serving, or do they reflect the character of Jesus? We may need to change our priorities; some of us might have to pick up the pace, others may have been shadow-boxing or straying off course. Some of us need to join the race! Let's pray and ask the Holy Spirit to put purpose in every stride as we run straight for the goal—the free gift of eternal life.

This poem was written by two young friends who know what it means to have hope.

The Race

When there is a burden on my shoulders,
I like to take a walk inside my mind,
But find it doesn't go far enough.
So I turn and run with others
Looking for the finish line,
And realize it's too far.

I try and run with some,
But they stumble and fall.
Their legs are weak and often stall.
I pull them to their feet.
As we run, the ground hardens with each step.
This one needs help,
But for this race I have not trained.

I will be back to strengthen these weak and
    stumbling limbs.
I go to my Coach and ask
For strength that I need to go on running.

The laps I run will be many
But His love is plenty.
As I run with grace
I pass many a life's disgrace.
In this never-ending race my legs are strong;
I will now conquer wrong.
I turn to the one on the hard ground
Telling him what I've found.

We run a slow pace

Filled with Hope

But our strides begin to fill with grace.
In no time we have run this race
And found we've won it sure and strong.
As you run this lifelong race,
Don't forget your Master's grace.
Or you shall stumble on your face!

What a great reminder that we can depend on "the Coach" to fill our lives with hope that we might continue the race. Life's waves of trials, failures, and tragedies will continue to roll into our lives, but Jesus Christ promises to give us hope and strength to continue the ride until we reach the ultimate goal, the shores of heaven. Wow! What a hope!

To order additional copies or to contact Tom Eggum to speak to your group write:

Tom Eggum Communications
P.O. Box 5268
Glendale, AZ 85312
602-978-1719